Management Lessons from Oz

Leading from Courage

Paul S. Zygielbaum

Cover art and design by Patrice LePera

www.leadingfromcourage.com

ISBN: 1533628718

ISBN 13: 978-1533628718

DEDICATION

This book is dedicated to my wife, Michelle. She has been my partner in life, co-conspirator, cheerleader, patient coach, and sometimes, caregiver. She has shared my Yellow Brick Road, and I hers. Sometimes she has needed my help climbing the hills, but most often I have needed hers. Mostly, she has been very tolerant and forbearing of my foibles, and I could not have reached this point without her.

CONTENTS

FOREWORD

As the saying goes, "some people come into our lives for a reason, for a season, or for a lifetime."

When Paul came into our corporate life at a major aerospace company, the reason was clear. I was a young executive and proud to admit that we needed help to take our performance to the next level! As the best consultants often do, Paul provided not only thorough analysis and sage counsel, but also practical "how to" recommendations, and what only a few great consultants do, the "people" insight, spiced up with the necessary dose of courage to make it stick!

Soon I knew that Paul had come into our corporate life not just for a "reason," but for a full "season," what I like to call my team's "growing pains" season. We discovered, experimented, implemented and learned together. Along the way, Paul became more and more an integral member of our team, and together we achieved what few teams had before in service of this great country and our brave men and women who keep us safe and at the forefront of innovation and technology.

Years later, I realized that Paul was going to be a friend for a lifetime. And his courage, reflecting a central theme of this book, would be on full display in a personal and painful way for himself, his family and those of us who are his friends. We have spent countless hours discussing among other things, *courage*, how it differs with *fearlessness*, and the degree of its relevance to great leadership.

As Maya Angelou best put it: *"Courage is the most important of all the virtues, because without courage you can't practice any other virtue consistently. You can practice any virtue erratically, but nothing consistently without courage."*

I agreed to write this Foreword to Paul's book because I believe that the central theme of this book around courage, the practical guidance throughout, and the emphasis on the "people" aspect, set it apart and make it a "must read" for leaders of all kinds and all ages, everywhere. I love the clever references to the Wizard of Oz. For those familiar with the story, what better character than the Cowardly Lion who sought courage?

Sonya Sepahban
Senior Vice President, General Dynamics (Retired)
February 2016

A LOOK BEHIND THE CURTAIN

"I can't come back! I don't know how it works!"
– The Wizard of Oz

"How many ways can you explain something to people?" snapped the corporate vice president, his exasperation simmering. He was overseeing the construction of new facilities for integrating and testing communications satellites, the shutdown of the old facility, and the coming layoff of 3,000 employees.

We sat on brown leather sofas, facing each other across a coffee table in the sitting area of his enormous office, inside the California headquarters of one of the world's leading aerospace/defense companies. Outside, it was a beautiful day in the spring of 1997, but his office lacked windows, for reasons of security, I imagined.

We were already two hours into this discussion, when I'd asked for only a 45-minute private meeting to talk about the general unrest and, particularly, the distrust of him that I'd encountered in his organization.

This talk wasn't strictly part of my consulting work to improve the company's communications satellite integration and test processes,

1

but I knew that it was impossible for my work to be successful if I didn't understand the situation more fully. Being my first meeting with him, this was also a chance for me to gain his trust, and perhaps to gain influence toward the success of my project and more business to follow.

Responding to the man's frustration as constructively as I could in the moment, I asked, "How have you tried?" Not for the first time in my career, I was beginning to feel less like a consultant and more like a therapist.

"I've talked with all the managers," he replied with a laugh, as if this were the correct answer.

So arrived an opportunity to become an advisor to this man, who reported to the chairman and CEO of one of the world's largest companies. It called for a lesson in leadership. "You have to reach beyond them to talk with the workers directly."

"I can't talk with three thousand people," he protested. It wasn't the employees to be laid off that he ought to have been worried about, so much as those who would remain.

"You don't have to," I said. "You only have to talk with enough of them that the word gets around. And the most you can do for those three thousand people is to let them know they've been listened to. Those who remain will need to know it."

"How do I do that?"

"Sit down and have lunch with fifteen or twenty employees from various parts of the organization. Do that four or five times with different groups. Speak honestly, listen to them, and show that you care. The word will get around."

He looked at the coffee table silently for a moment. Then his shoulders sagged, and his expression sank to one of defeat. "I don't think I'm gonna survive this."

I didn't really know whether he meant professionally or physically, which was troubling, but there was no doubt that I had won his trust. Despite the business possibilities that might have derived from that fact, I was immediately certain that he wouldn't last more than sixty days in his job. I couldn't stop my lips from pursing for a moment.

Anyway, it was time for me to leave for my next appointment, which happened to be with one of his competitors. But this was still a good opportunity for me to learn something more about executive management and about this company. I softened my voice. "Tell me something," I asked. "You report to the CEO. In his staff meetings, do you ever discuss the organization's values or culture?"

"No. It's all about the numbers."

I nodded, stood, thanked him for his time, and apologized for the meeting taking longer than I'd requested.

"Oh, no," he said, walking me to the door of his office. He looked me in the eye as he shook my hand. "It's nice to have someone to talk to."

He lasted thirty days.

WE'RE OFF TO SEE THE WIZARD

"It's always best to start at the beginning.
And all you do is follow the Yellow Brick Road."
– Glinda

Why Does this Book Exist?

This book is about simple things. Things so simple that they form the basis of a children's story. Things so profound that the story is beloved by everyone and quoted remarkably often.

I'm referring to the movie "The Wizard of Oz," the 1939 Warner Brothers production starring Judy Garland and other wonderful actors. Plenty of Americans, at least, have seen the movie. It gives us a common experience, language and symbolism to utilize in the discussion of leadership. Not to worry if you don't know the story, because a synopsis is contained in Appendix C.

The idea for using these fundamentals to teach about leadership came to me while I was serving as chief operating officer of C8 MediSensors, a company that I'd co-founded. The company had been operating for almost nine years and was preparing to file for regulatory approval to introduce our revolutionary medical device to our first market, in Europe. The investors were keenly awaiting that filing. The device was a wearable, non-invasive, continuous monitor for blood glucose for use by diabetes patients and for other medical applications. The potential global market constituted hundreds of millions of people and innumerable hospitals and medical clinics. In the dozens of previous attempts by others, no one had ever been closer to having a successful non-invasive glucose monitor. Our innovative spectrographic hardware platform could be adapted to many other industrial and commercial uses as well.

From the outside, the company appeared to stand on the verge of becoming a stupendous Silicon Valley success story and a godsend to hundreds of millions of patients around the world.

However, things had deteriorated in recent months. We were still facing some technical difficulties that threatened the product launch schedule. We were almost out of cash, with certain unsympathetic investors ready to pounce with proposals for diluting the stock and taking control of the company. We had ramped up production capacity and increased hiring in anticipation of a large, lucrative deal that didn't materialize. As a result, we were facing furloughs among our amazing employees and termination of important consulting contracts, something that pained me deeply. There was fear and grave internal strife among the executive staff, and this was reflected in dissention among the various departments. The path forward for the company was uncertain and full of deadly hazards.

In March of 2012, against this backdrop, the CEO, my long-time friend and co-founder, was brought down by a medical condition. I had to step in to run the company temporarily. As it happened, I was appointed CEO about a month later.

Arranging new corporate financing was critically important in the short run, but I knew that my most important task for the longer term was to get the executive team functioning smoothly and seamlessly, and driving this transformation throughout the organization, as quickly as possible.

In my first week running the company, my nearly 40 years of management experience and education told me what to do to get things moving in the right direction with my staff. It happened in that odd way that people sometimes relate. I awoke in the middle of the night after a rather vivid dream, and after just a few moments, the whole idea unfolded and arranged itself in my mind: *All the key lessons in leadership that I'd learned over the years were symbolized by Dorothy's journey and the key characters who helped her along her way.* I shared these ideas with my staff the next day and utilized them as a rallying cry to move us forward. It worked. In this book, I will share the same ideas with you.

By the end of that year, C8 MediSensors was awaiting only the resolution of some technical issues that had shown up in the clinical trials of our device and were delaying our product launch. Lack of cash was again an immediate problem facing us.

Despite the stress, I knew by then that I loved my job. I was achieving organizational success by applying the leadership lessons I'd learned over my entire career.

I'll tell you presently how things worked out. Let's say, for now, that the outcome is a reminder that nothing is certain in this world, and that leadership demands courage in the face of that uncertainty.

In the end, I achieved my lifelong dream of leading a cutting-edge technological organization. My second retirement has given me the opportunity to reflect on the lessons of a long and varied career in leadership. I want to share what I've learned along my path. That's why this book exists.

The Yellow Brick Road of an Aspiring Leader

I think it was my father who unwittingly set me on my own Yellow Brick Road, when I was just nine years old.

My father worked at Caltech's Jet Propulsion Laboratory (JPL) in the 1950s and '60s and was directly involved in the development of Explorer I, America's first successful space satellite. After the Soviets launched Sputnik I, he became engaged in surveillance and intelligence work regarding Soviet space and military programs during those fearsome times. On many evenings, he and my mother would host small cocktail parties at our home, which would be attended by various JPL executives and their wives.

On those special evenings, I would take advantage of my status as a small, ignorable boy to listen in on their heady discussions of technical and organizational issues. *What makes these people tick?* I wondered. *How do they make their decisions? How did they become who they are?*

What I could sense mostly was the excitement and enthusiasm that these men had for their mission, and the unwavering courage that they brought to their roles as leaders. I began to visualize myself as someone like them when I was grown. It became my dream to be among the leaders of an organization that would create cutting-edge technologies and bring them to fruition. At first, I wanted it to be in the aerospace industry, but much later, my perspective broadened: It wasn't the specific technology or industry that drew me, but the role of leadership. Like Dorothy, I had my quest.

Thus, I have always considered myself a student of management processes, of leadership processes. I have observed managers from bottom to top of many companies in four commercial industries, among profit and non-profit organizations and government agencies, in lean times and fat times, and in the US and other countries. Over the 40-plus years of my career, I've observed an astounding number of ineffective managers, a lot I would consider mediocre, and relatively few really insightful, wise, courageous leaders.

Let me give you a peek at the route that my Yellow Brick Road followed. It took me in 1968 to Caltech, the California Institute of Technology, where I pursued a challenging education primarily in engineering, physics, math, and humanities, along with a strong dose of recreation that would bear another book for the telling. While there, I took a job, first as a technician and later as an engineer, in JPL's Propulsion Division. So I was off to a good start. In 1973, newly married, I gained my Master's Degree.

I moved on to an aerospace manufacturing company for a short time, but then, in the wake of the OPEC oil embargo, I was lured to the electric utility industry to manage R&D programs in advanced power generation and energy storage technologies for the newly formed Electric Power Research Institute (EPRI).

After 8 years of that, I decided to shift my career to an industry with faster product life cycles, for the learning that it would offer. I joined a division of Hewlett Packard (HP) that produced test equipment for the electronic communications industry, and I spent the next 21 years learning about leading manufacturing operations and business in general, and in the practice of consulting to executives of other companies. In 2003 I left that part of my career behind and moved into private consulting for a time.

I tried to retire when faced with cancer treatment in 2004, but as things progressed, a couple of my old Caltech buddies convinced me to join them in a worthy medical device startup, C8 MediSensors. I eventually spent about nine years with that company, finishing as CEO. Finally, I got to retire again at the end of 2012. Like Dorothy,

I was happy to be home again, having learned what I needed to.

I'll tell you more of my adventures on this Yellow Brick Road later on.

Who Ought to Read this Book?

Over the years, I have found my experiences to offer useful teaching points to colleagues and friends in various circumstances. Some of these colleagues have been other executives or managers within my own organizations, some were consulting clients, and many were subordinates or simply friends. Some have been politicians in office or seeking office.

Because this book is about the qualities of effective leadership, it tends to cite experiences with executives and managers within sizable organizations. After all, those kinds of organizations have dominated my professional career.

But the lessons about leadership are universal. They can be applied in large or small companies, in political settings, or simply within a family. The insights can be applied by organizational leaders and can provide perspective for the people who work for those leaders, whether as employees or independent contractors. The work world continues to evolve, but where leadership is concerned, the more it changes, the more it stays the same.

So I think that this book is for organizational leaders, anyone who aspires to leadership, and members of organizations who want to learn how to relate to their leaders more effectively. Draw what you need from it.

How Will Our Journey Proceed?

It's said that stories are the best way to convey lessons, and I believe that's true. As you go through this book, you will read stories of my encounters with leaders and others that are meant to illustrate leadership principles. These are real reminiscences from my career, related as accurately as I can recall, but modified slightly in some cases, in order to protect individual identities where appropriate. The companies that are identified in the text represent just a few of the hundreds of organizations with which I've had the pleasure of interacting over the years. The challenges that they faced and the shortcomings that they exhibited, as recounted here, are representative but by no means unique to them.

One note on terminology. *Management* and *leadership* are overlapping principles, but they are certainly different concepts. Many definitions are available for both words. I think of a leader as being a person who articulates a set of values, a corresponding vision of the future and a corresponding mission to be accomplished, and who inspires and organizes others to join in that accomplishment. I think of a manager, in contrast, as someone who organizes effort within the mission. Note that these are definitions of functions rather than capabilities, as one would hope that every manager has the potential to be a leader. These definitions could certainly be refined and embellished, but I think they communicate the fundamental difference for our purpose here.

Throughout this book, I have chosen the use of those two words, or forms of them, for clarity and maximum meaning within the local context. It could be argued that *leader* and *leadership* might be chosen in all cases, because that quality is what, ideally, we seek to find in every manager, and not just the relatively mundane capability of getting things done through others. But sometimes in the text, I'm referring to the person's organizational slot, where *manager* and *management* are the clearer terms.

As Dorothy proceeded along her path of discovery, she acquired her friends one at a time, revealing a fundamental truth about her quest with each one. We shall do likewise:

- In "The Scarecrow," we will discover something of the knowledge and wisdom that a leader needs. Much of that discussion focuses on the manufacturing environment, but the processes of uncovering and applying knowledge and wisdom in a leadership role are universal. And Appendix A presents my associated theory of how to view the development of a product or service as a series of planned risk reductions, and what this implies about how development programs ought to be managed.
- In "The Tin Man," we will explore the role of love and compassion in unleashing the creative, collaborative, productive forces that often lie latent in an organization.
- In "The Cowardly Lion," we will examine the role and structure of courage, which seems the least well-defined and analyzed quality of organizational leadership.
- In "Dorothy," we will distill the fundamental lessons about these qualities that every leader ought to understand, and we'll point the way toward applying these lessons in different business leadership roles, by means of the corollary material in Appendix B.
- Finally, in "The Wizard," we will reach our goal, only to find, like Dorothy, that what we achieve may be something other than what we had sought.

This book aims to contribute to the conversation about leadership and, especially, about courage in leadership. I sincerely hope you find value in the messages in these pages. This is not a how-to book. It's about the concepts. Your Yellow Brick Road will not be anyone else's. It will be your own, so find your own way. But please go carefully. To paraphrase a cliché from the movie, you're not in Kansas anymore.

Just how did "The Wizard of Oz" become our template? Let's find out.

INTO THE CYCLONE

"We must be up inside the cyclone."
— Dorothy

The date was March 26, 2012, a Monday. I awoke in a cold sweat. The clock said it was 3:30 a.m., but the vestige of a dream kept me from understanding that fully. I felt as if I had been in a meeting at work, and the word *courage* was stuck in my head.

It had been one of those vivid dreams, the kind that feels like real talking, real moving, real interaction. Just after the meeting ended and just before I woke up, someone had said to me, "They just need the courage." The place and the people had been familiar but not exactly those I knew. But who, where? It was already getting fuzzy.

C8 MediSensors was in trouble. Running short of cash, the board angry, investors clamoring, mistrust among the executive staff. We were getting remarkably close to success with a technology that no one had believed was even possible, but things seemed to be unraveling. Like the Paul Simon song said, "The nearer your destination, the more you're slip-sliding away."

It had been just a week since I'd had to step, at least temporarily, into the shoes of our CEO, Dr. Robert P. McNamara. He was home recovering from a medical emergency. He was my good friend and co-founder, and he had been my college housemate back when Paul Simon and Art Garfunkel were making their best music together. Our third co-founder, Dr. Jan Lipson, another college housemate and the CTO and primary inventor of our technology, had died in a terrible bicycling accident just a couple of years earlier. It seemed like all the fair winds of our early startup days, all the startling coincidences and circumstances that had propelled us forward, had been swallowed by a cyclone. And we were all caught in it.

I moved the blanket and sheets off, as quietly as I could, so as not to disturb my wife next to me. I continued to perspire.

They just need the courage. Courage.

A ludicrous image appeared in my mind, an old and familiar furry mask. An actor in a funny, endearing lion's suit. Bert Lahr. The Cowardly Lion. "Courage," he said.

Our company had a one-page "statement of values," one of those things that every good company ought to have. And we had strong values, indeed. The three of us had agreed that we would try to set the example of a company with an ethical and moral code to be admired. We would be among the leaders in how we treated employees, and we believed that we had achieved that to a large measure. We would set a standard for dealing with customers and suppliers in the medical device industry. We would be strong citizens of our community. I had agreed to serve as COO on the condition that our business model would enable us eventually to give away our product and support it in the Third World, and it appeared that we could make it so. We were proud. We were determined. We were going to change the world for the better.

Our statement of values included these seven concepts: intention and commitment, integrity, performance, individual dignity and growth, boldness, healthy living, and community. We defined each one in our own way. I hadn't given these a lot of thought lately.

It came to me, lying there drying off, that the word *courage* appeared on that page, but not as a value itself. Interesting. We defined *boldness* as the courage to do things in unconventional ways. Well, boldness is close to courage, isn't it?

Thinking I ought to go back to sleep, I pondered instead.

Whom did Dorothy encounter along her Yellow Brick Road? A Scarecrow who craved a brain, a Tin Man who wished for a heart, and a Cowardly Lion who sought courage. But each of those characters demonstrated that he had those very attributes all along, as the Wizard later pointed out. So Dorothy had those resources with her along her way.

What about Dorothy? Well, she was on a mission. She wanted to go home. She harped on it. She whined about it. She pestered everyone about it. Dorothy never forgot her mission for one minute, the whole damned movie!

My mind zeroed in on my staff.

R&D didn't have the data they needed yet, so they couldn't say when we'd solve the remaining technical issues or when we could launch the product. And they didn't know when they'd have that data, either.

Manufacturing was struggling with the problem of improving product consistency without being able to build enough products to drive that improvement properly.

Marketing was pushing out the launch schedule and had concerns about the potential impact on sales and the marketing infrastructure.

Regulatory was struggling to get ready to file with the European authorities for approval of our product for sale, and they weren't yet confident in the strength of the information we had.

Finance was pointing to the cash account and sending me distress signals.

And there was general grumbling about how certain folks didn't seem to be on the same page.

Down the chain of the organization, seams were fraying. There were arguments without solutions. There were unkind accusations. There was a lot of wheel-spinning and not a lot of smooth process.

Everyone seemed afraid, and I couldn't blame them.

Things hadn't been so bad earlier. Not great, but working. However, the stress had been building. And the sudden change at the top seemed to bring it all to a head.

I was sure that I would make a deal with investors for the financing we needed. It would be ugly, but we'd keep going, I was confident.

But my 40 years of management experience, line and staff, first-level to executive, told me that if I didn't get my executive team working smoothly very quickly, we didn't have a prayer of success.

I had a staff meeting scheduled for that afternoon. I made a decision.

My mind relaxed, and I went back to sleep.

***

It was another long day, and through all the meetings and discussions, I anticipated my 4:30 pm staff meeting with a mix of eagerness and trepidation. Shortly before, I printed copies of our statement of values for the entire staff, went into our board room, and laid a copy in front of each chair. I hooked up my laptop computer to show the same page on the projection screen as well. Then I waited for everyone to come in.

I wondered if they'd like what I had to say, if they'd embrace it, or if they'd think I had gone crazy and just lose whatever confidence they had left.

People filtered in. The CFO; the CTO; the VPs of Research and Development, Finance and Human Resources, Manufacturing, Marketing, Regulatory and Clinical, and Information Technology; and the Program Manager. It was my habit to start meetings on time, and I was pleased that everyone had arrived to hear my opening.

"Everyone has a copy of our values statement in front of them," I said. There were smiles and questioning looks. This wasn't how I'd started the multiple staff meetings of the past tumultuous week.

"I want to ask you all a question." I paused to collect their attention. "What's the most important word on this page?"

Some people looked incredulous. Others started to look at the papers in front of them or at the screen. A few answers popped up. "Excellence." "Commitment." "Empowering." Then a few more. Each person had his or her own idea. No one said the answer that I had in mind. A few moments passed in silence.

"Courage," I said, trying not to sound like Bert Lahr. I paused while everyone found that word on the page. Then I continued. "It takes courage to be a manager. You have to get up in the morning and know that you're coming into the office to deal with whatever difficult problems there are, whether technical or financial or human or whatever. You know that you have to make good decisions. It's hard to be a manager, and it takes courage."

There were nods and a few murmurs of assent.

"I don't know why we didn't make courage one of our values, but it's the most important word on that page. And the interesting thing for me is that it's the one qualification for management that I don't think is mentioned in any management textbook I've ever seen. Maybe you can't teach courage. I don't know. But it's the first thing all of us have to have."

Then I went for broke. "I had a dream last night, about courage. And it got me to thinking about the Cowardly Lion." There wasn't a person in the room who didn't smile. So I knew we had a cultural link that we could use.

"And that got me to thinking about Dorothy and all the rest. And you know what's interesting? I think L. Frank Baum was a genius. Because here's what he said. Dorothy was on a mission. She wanted to go home. She did not lose sight of that mission for one minute, not for one minute." A few nods, and a few questioning looks. *Where is this guy heading with this?* they were thinking.

"And whom did she take with her on her quest? The Scarecrow, who represented knowledge and wisdom. The Tin Man, who represented love and compassion." Now some were giving me skeptical looks, especially the technical guys, but our VP of Finance and HR was smiling. "And the Cowardly Lion, who was courage.

Those are the things she needed."

I let it sink in for a moment, and then I continued. "We're on a mission. Every one of you is here because you have the knowledge and wisdom that this company needs to succeed. You're the only team in the world that does! And you wouldn't be here if you didn't have the love and compassion to devote yourselves to developing a medical device that will benefit hundreds of millions of people."

Nods all around the table. They were proud, and justifiably so. By aligning with that pride, I had completed the setup for my real message.

"What you also need to bring with you is your courage. I need you to bring your courage. Without it, we won't be successful."

I let that stay in the air for a moment. No one was arguing, and no one seemed to think I was crazy.

"I know that we have a lot of issues in front of us. A lot of problems to solve." Nods again. Everyone was dead serious and engaged now.

"And there are a lot of things we want that we don't have." More nods. "But you know what? It turns out that Dorothy had the means to get home with her all the time. The ruby slippers. She had what she needed the whole time." Again, I let it stand, and there were smiles and nods, which pleased me.

I summed up with my call to action. "We're on a mission. I'm counting on your knowledge, wisdom, love, compassion, and courage. And you have what you have to work with. Make it do."

Now, I will not say that there was a great change in that moment.

The scene didn't shift from sepia tones to Technicolor®, like it did when Dorothy landed in Oz. But I perceived a subtle change. People were thoughtful. Some smiled. Some nodded. They were quiet.

It was the moment, I think, that most of them realized that the many problems they had among them would require their courage to resolve, and that I wasn't going to settle for less.

After another moment, I moved us on to the business of the day.

***

How did it work out? We got the funds to move forward. They would trickle in, but if we performed on schedule, we would survive to get to market. We filed with the European regulatory authorities a few weeks later, after a monumental, day-and-night effort by our staff. Within a couple of months, most of the internal strife was gone. The team was focused on a clear set of objectives, plans were jointly worked out, and progress was tracked intently. There were still disagreements among members of the organization, naturally, but the processes for resolving them were becoming steadily healthier.

The company's working atmosphere and results improved apace. By November, I recognized that I was no longer needed to lead the decision processes of the executive team. They knew how to do it, and I became more of an advisor and an ultimate arbiter for them. I was mostly a spectator at my staff meetings in December, although I'm not sure that the staff recognized that.

Although we had furloughed many of our employees, the vast majority of the rest remained staunchly loyal and was working hard to make us successful. Decision processes and execution of plans among the departments were happening consistently well.

We received our European regulatory approval in October, after an agonizing bureaucratic delay. This approval gave us the right to sell our devices in 26 countries, and our plan was to begin sales as soon as we had clinical test results that satisfied our own strict performance standard.

A celebration was in order. My wife picked up the two cases of Veuve Clicquot Ponsardin champagne that had been chilling for weeks in anticipation, and she brought them to our suitably futuristic headquarters building in south San Jose. The entire active company staff and consultants gathered to toast this tremendous business milestone.

I desperately wanted to see the company through to a technological and commercial triumph. After all, I was a potential customer myself, and I wanted everyone like me to have access to our wonderful new technology. My wife and I were major investors in the company as well. And I wanted our employees to be part of a great Silicon Valley success, a yearning that I could read in their eyes. Moreover, they all had stock options, and some had exercised those and become shareholders, too.

I figured that I had a few months of work before me to see to the resolution of the remaining operational issues that had my attention. Regrettably, I didn't get that chance.

I had been facing my own serious medical issues and had told the Board of Directors months earlier that I would have to step down as soon as we had identified a suitable replacement. I left the CEO position at the end of December, after we hired an excellent replacement, Mr. John Kaiser, who had a long, illustrious history in the diabetes medical device industry. He came out of retirement for the fourth time to lead us, with great excitement at our prospects.

After enduring one of the most stressful episodes of my professional career, and despite continued financial duress for the company, I knew that the team as a whole was operating reasonably efficiently and effectively. I was proud of the team and what we had accomplished, and I was fully confident that, with sufficient financial resources behind them, the team would be very successful. And I was rather confident that John would raise the necessary funds.

I accepted John's request that I stay on with the simple title of Co-Founder, to advise and assist him as the company moved forward. We were already in agreement on the main points, and he was exceptionally well-positioned to proceed. But the end of this story is most sad and stunning: John passed away just five weeks later as the result of a sporting accident, and the company collapsed.

***

Not every story has a happy ending. But the staff meeting in which I'd presented my Oz analogy ultimately proved to be the first step on a journey that was successful in bringing forth the courage of the team, as well as the best of its knowledge, wisdom, love and compassion. Despite the unfortunate outcome of the company's journey, I will always be proud of the ways in which the leadership team displayed those very qualities, with fierce determination and dedication to our mission.

I choose to hope that this shared experience yielded valuable lessons for each member of the team, as we continued our individual journeys along our own Yellow Brick Roads.

THE SCARECROW

"Gosh, it would be awful pleasin'
To reason out the reason
For things I can't explain."
— The Scarecrow

Dorothy finds him in a cornfield, hanging from a post. He is helpless to stop the crows from pulling straw from his body. He believes that his lack of a brain makes him helpless. But he knows enough to suggest that Dorothy free him by bending the nail that holds him in place. What else does he not realize that he knows, and what wisdom is in him?

The First Stop on My Yellow Brick Road

Before we discuss some points of knowledge and wisdom involved in being a business leader, I'll walk you down a bit of my Yellow Brick Road. As I stated earlier, I started out wanting a career in aerospace. I was aware that most of those JPL executives that I'd rubbed elbows with as a nine-year-old (or would have, had I been tall enough) had held degrees in physics or engineering. So I earned my bachelor's degree from Caltech in engineering and applied science, with a specialty in jet propulsion. ("Jet" was a legacy from the olden days when "rocket" was not considered respectable.) I recall that I was also just two courses shy of the requirement for a bachelor's degree in physics, although Caltech didn't offer dual bachelor's degrees. I followed up there with a master's degree in mechanical engineering.

I had basically created my own, broad-based major that covered not only propulsion, aerodynamics and trajectory analysis, but also structural engineering, advanced physics, and an overdose of applied mathematics as well. It was, perhaps, a precursor to Caltech's modern aerospace engineering curriculum. However, I found, perhaps not surprisingly, that my best grades generally came in courses related to management, labor relations and the humanities.

This is not to say that I was an outstanding student at Caltech as measured by grades, perhaps because, by my sophomore year, I was working about 20 hours per week as a technician in the Propulsion Division of JPL, which gradually extended to 40 hours per week after I got my degree and became a full-fledged engineer. And meanwhile I worked 10-20 hours per week in my parents' bakery on the other side of the Los Angeles basin, just to help them. I'm not complaining, just explaining what my undergraduate advisor called my "fairly mediocre" record. So there I was, after years of intense effort, still feeling like the Scarecrow in search of a brain.

I was fortunate to have a kind professor of fluid mechanics and dynamics, the late Professor Rolf Sabersky, who supported my application to stay on for the master's degree. By then I was engaged to Michelle, a most lovely, astute and forbearing woman. She also proved to be an academic miracle, as my grades soared that year. Well, mostly. I barely made it through advanced probability theory, by virtue of another kind professor. In the decades since, the terror of mid-term and final exams has faded, and I am left with a lot of fond memories of those days. I will never forget the kindness of those professors, who lived up to the lesson that the Tin Man eventually learned from the Wizard, "...that a heart is not judged by how much you love, but by how much you are loved by others."

With that, let's come back and commune with the Scarecrow.

Knowing What the Job Is

It was 1988, and I was sitting in one of those off-site management retreats at HP, a two-day ordeal for the purpose of redefining our division's mission statement while building teamwork. One of those things that makes some people glad that they're not managers. Still, there was a lot of value in the discussion, some of which was just about definitions of terms. One of the most memorable exchanges, for me, was a brief, unfinished discussion about exactly what we managed.

I was a manufacturing product line manager, with engineering, marketing and production responsibility, in HP's Microwave Technology Division, a world-leading source of component technology for use in HP's communications test and measurement equipment products. That group of divisions formed a very profitable business, with about a billion dollars in annual revenue back then. Our division was a key enabler of that success, but we had competitive challenges from outside the company. So several dozen managers were gathered to address how best to move forward, and this had to begin with clarification of our purpose and objectives.

The management team's resumes included a plethora of doctorates in electrical engineering, physics and other technical fields. They were rightfully proud of the division's technical accomplishments, but I could not say that all of these managers employed the most effective techniques for leading people.

The discussion during the retreat was focused and intense. Partway into the first day, one of the R&D managers had made a comment that our division's purpose was to manage technologies for HP's Test and Measurement business. By the word *manage*, I think he meant making decisions about technologies to develop in-house, and then exploiting and enhancing them to the fullest through their life cycles. A bit later, I had countered that our job was rather *to lead people* who produced those technologies. Thereby began a brief debate that seemed to have, at its root, a disagreement on how we viewed our jobs.

Over time, through my experiences in driving turn-arounds of groups within that division and in other settings, I learned that one cannot divorce technology, products, processes and people when architecting an organization. Changes in one aspect will affect the others, and the best leaders are able to coordinate changes in all these aspects so as to achieve the desired results. So, I would acknowledge that our business purpose at the time was to manage technologies for HP, but I would still contend that we accomplished that by leading people who produced those technologies. The "what" and the "how" were intimately related, and our skills in leading people were as critical to success as those people's technical ability to invent and develop technologies.

In this particular respect, *leadership* and *management* are identical. As my good friend, Ms. Sonya Sepahban, has written to me, these roles are "…all about people, knowing them, reading them, helping them be the best they can be, listening to them, learning from them. So many times this is overlooked when promoting managers/leaders, especially in large corporations, where quarter-over-quarter numbers are king."[1] Her words could well be the career epitaph of that aerospace corporate vice president whose lack of understanding I related at the beginning of this book. I would add that these skills are best learned early in a leader's career, when the consequences of a mistake are generally of small scale. This is not something to be understood just by leaders of great organizations, but also by first-line supervisors and everyone in between. A useful beginning point for formal study in this area is the Emotional Intelligence model, first suggested by psychologists John Mayer and Peter Salovey[2] and later articulated in a well-known book by Daniel Goleman.[3] This model has been further expanded by others, as well.

But when you step into a management job, just how do you know what to do first?

Knowing Which Knobs to Turn

Whether taking charge of an operation as its leader or walking through a previously unseen factory in an effort to sell my consulting services, I always had the sense that I was standing in front of an enormous control panel that I didn't immediately understand. I imagined a wall full of knobs, switches, meters, dials and lights that looked intimidating, because I didn't understand their individual functions or how they interrelated.

I knew that the factory wasn't running as best it might, and I knew that there were many knobs and switches that I could manipulate that wouldn't make any significant difference to that. But I also believed that there were a few controls that, if I could just identify them, might be tweaked to move things in the right direction. My job was to identify those and figure out just how to move them.

Those knobs and switches, by the way, might affect technology, products, processes, and people. It would be foolish to think that I could be successful by picking only one or two of these aspects.

It always took a good deal of fact-finding and analysis to pick just the few controls to tweak, and how to adjust them. Quite often, the answer turned out to include some combination of product design changes to make it more manufacturable, upgrades to manufacturing and test processes, improved utilization of information from test, and revised metrics and incentives applied to groups and even individuals. That meant turning several knobs, usually, but not a great number, and they had to be adjusted in a well-planned, timely, coordinated fashion. That's where the complexity arose.

The point is, while I had an unusual perspective on organizations and technologies as a result of my particular experiences, it is always valuable to choose just a few things to change, and just those few that can be expected to move things measurably in the desired direction.

Well, in a manufacturing company, or a software company, or even in a consulting firm, everything begins with product development. If you let your imagination run a bit, you can also see that this is true in a community service organization, a political party, or practically any other organization. Sometimes it's a "service" rather than a "product," but the concepts are the same. So let's talk about that first. Being a manufacturing kind of guy, I'll address this topic in that language.

Product Development and Business Risk

In 2005 I was in Tucson, Arizona, making my final presentation of results to the executive staff of Raytheon Missile Systems, which manufactures various military missiles. The Raytheon vice president in charge of Missile Systems had sought my consultancy on how to improve profitability in the production phases of missile programs. Perhaps a dozen people sat around a conference table, intent upon my words, as I had painted a very bleak picture of their present situation for them.

While missile development then was always a cost-plus arrangement, whereby the company made a satisfactory pre-determined profit percentage on the development cost, the production phase was fixed-price, with some discounts for order volume. This meant that if the company's manufacturing and test processes cost more than the company had predicted during development, the company stood to lose money on every missile they shipped, or at least to make far less profit than they'd hoped.

The development phase generally ended after a demonstrator missile satisfactorily tracked and destroyed a test target. I picture generals or admirals, and a few politicians, shaking hands with company executives, and procurement officers signing papers to begin missile production. At that point, the company hopes to make a fair profit on future orders, but often it doesn't turn out so.

And such was Raytheon's dilemma. They were consistently making far less money on missile manufacturing than they'd predicted, and it was hurting their business severely, in several ways. Based on work that I'd already done in the company's satellite-related business, these people were hoping that I could offer them some insight on how to improve profitability in production.

I had necessarily extended my process investigations and analysis into the product development processes, as well as the various production steps involved in missile manufacturing, integration and test, because the root of profitability issues in production is often to be found in the R&D operation.

I had examined five different missile programs and had created an analytical model of the factory processes, and my model predicted production costs rather accurately. This gave me the ability to examine the anticipated effects of potential process changes on profitability.

I had found that the development programs were not accurately predicting production costs because they were typically underestimating the risks that remained to be resolved at each phase of the development, including at the time of release to production. This meant that the production operation was "eating" these risks and paying the price. There were certainly some gains to be made in missile integration and test processes in production, but the major part of the solution for future programs would be to change the development processes so as to better recognize and reduce risks prior to entering production.

The depth of the problem was amply illustrated during my presentation, when I was presenting the concept of product development as a risk-reduction process. The vice president, seeing quizzical looks from his staff that apparently mirrored his own puzzlement, stopped me and said, "We don't understand what you mean by the word *risk*." I asked him what they thought that word meant. "Well, we use it to mean the risk that the demonstrator doesn't hit the target," he said.

A bit flustered, I'm afraid I replied rather brusquely. "The demonstrator pretty much always hits the target eventually, doesn't it? I'm talking about the risk that you won't hit your production cost target when you start production. That's the problem you hired me to solve." With that new understanding, we moved on to an excellent discussion and action plan.

My definition of *risk* in the context of that project seemed a revelation to that audience, and the fact that this risk was not being managed adequately during product development seemed startling to them. When I thought about this later in comparison to my other experiences with product development processes, I decided that theirs was not an extraordinary perspective at the time, but rather a common one.

In the time that has passed since then, I still have not seen any other analysis of product development specifically as a risk-reduction process. But the Scarecrow will not be denied. Since the detailed discussion is rather long and dry, I have placed that into Appendix A, which I highly recommend for a fuller understanding. Here, we'll limit ourselves to some key points, simplified to their essence:

- Every organization that develops products has a process, or rather a set of processes, for doing so. Each product development program consists of a series of phases, climaxing with the release of the product for sale to customers.

- At the beginning, each program is characterized by what is already known about the product and its intended market, and what is not known. The things that are not known represent sources of business risk. As the development proceeds from phase to phase, building knowledge, the intention is to reduce the remaining risks by prescribed amounts, until those risks are small enough to be managed by the production organization, after release to production, in the normal course of business.

- Each phase release represents a review of progress against specific risk-reduction targets. If some targets for a particular release are not met at the time of the review, management can elect to move ahead into the next phase anyway, with the expectation that the exceptions will be resolved in a timely manner.

- Phase release meetings, which are meant to evaluate remaining business risk in a program in preparation for a decision to invest additional funds, must be viewed as business meetings, rather than technical reviews. This distinction is fundamental to how information ought to be presented and discussed.

- There is a danger that such reviews will be faulty, in the sense that some unresolved risks, or exceptions, will not be recognized. If this happens systemically, then the organization may well find itself unsatisfied with business results after the release to production, since risks invariably materialize in production as unacceptable costs.

- There can be several reasons for systemic error in regard to the estimation of remaining risk. These generally derive from the culture of the organization, which may stifle objective disclosure of remaining risks. It is up to the leaders of the organization to create an environment that encourages participants to speak even the harshest truth about the risks at hand. It ought not to take an act of exceptional courage for an employee or a manager to expose an unresolved risk, and one of the most important functions of leadership is to create an environment of low barriers to that kind of disclosure. *The courage ought to show in the leadership's intention, commitment and action to create such a culture. This is what we ought to expect of organizational leaders.*

In the case of Raytheon Missile Systems, I recommended a variety of changes aimed at implementing a lean development process, a strengthened strategy for testing and the use of information from test, and more robust organizational processes to unleash the team's creativity. These strategies were aimed largely at eliminating systemic error in the measurement of remaining risk during missile development. All of this was to be structured in a careful, choreographed implementation. The Raytheon leadership team adopted my recommendations.

It was all about knowing which knobs to turn and how, and about being able to motivate the team to make those changes. The

Scarecrow is in ascendance in these environs, but he must always be ably assisted by the Tin Man and the Cowardly Lion.

This is a good point to introduce some important lessons about product development that carry over into other realms.

The Value of Test

The VP of Manufacturing was walking me through his factory, one day in the late 1990s. His company produced electronic components used in microwave communications systems. I had been called in by his HP account manager, our salesman, to have a look at whether I might help this company improve its business results.

We were passing by one of their electronic test stations, and I observed a large amount of work-in-process inventory awaiting test. A number of engineers were gathered around the test system, talking with the test technician. There were a lot of frowns among the group.

The VP said something about how there was so much cost tied up in test and no value coming from it. I responded, "There's no value in testing?"

"Well, the only value is that it allows me to ship product. It's a screen for bad product. We can't ship without testing to make sure the product is good."

I'd heard comments in this vein so often from managers at various levels that I had developed a standard way of changing their minds. "Let me ask you a question. Do you train your people?"

"Of course."

"And what is training?"

"Providing information that helps our people do their jobs better."

"Exactly. And what is test?"

He remained silent, looking at me. Illumination began to fill his face.

I said, "The proper role of test in manufacturing is to provide information that drives the improvement of the processes and the product. If you're not using it for that, you are not getting the benefit from the investment."

A more formal definition would show that the value of test in production is composed of the reduction of all other costs of production, such as labor, capital investment, material scrap, and work-in-process inventory, as well as the much-coveted reduction of production cycle time. Customer returns may be reduced as well, and the favorable effects may also reflect back into more efficient product development. But I didn't need to explain this to this customer, as he was rather quick on the uptake.

"I know who you are!" he suddenly exclaimed, pointing his finger at me. He looked at the account manager and back at me. "You're the rainmaker!"

"At your service," I replied with a smile and a slight bow. "But I promise I won't sell you more rain than you really need."

In today's world, where more and more functions are moving from hardware to software, test becomes ever more important and offers increasing value. As electronic product life cycles continue to shrink, it's critical to ensure the integrity of hardware and software design and manufacturing very early. Imagine the cost burden that Apple suffered when they introduced their faulty first attempt at a map application for their iPhones®. Having your customers serve as your testers is a risky strategy to rely upon.

Is This a Business Meeting?

Earlier we discussed the business nature of phase release meetings. That is more properly a general observation not limited to product development.

Let me harken back to early 1978, the days of Osborne and Tandy computers, and the earliest Apples. It had been just four years since the OPEC oil embargo, and President Carter's Project Independence was busy failing. I was working as an R&D project manager for the Electric Power Research Institute (EPRI), but I had requested a loan assignment to a utility company in order to gain some practical field experience. So my position at the moment was that of a consulting startup engineer on a steam turbine power generation system in Oregon. This unit was part of a "combined cycle" power plant in which the steam for the turbine was created by heating water using the exhaust gas of several oil-fired gas turbines. The steam turbine had been added beside the existing gas turbines, and I had responsibility for overseeing the final installation and startup of some of its auxiliary systems.

The steam turbine system was guaranteed by the manufacturer to produce a certain minimum power output at a certain minimum thermodynamic efficiency. So part of the startup process was to test that performance, using a fuel efficiency metric called the "guaranteed heat rate." If the system failed the test, then the manufacturer would have to pay a substantial penalty to the utility company, according to the contract of sale. Millions of dollars were at stake.

A meeting was scheduled between the manufacturer's and utility's engineers to discuss the test procedure.

The plant engineering manager asked me to attend the meeting along with a couple of the other engineers, and I thought that would be interesting and educational.

The exact performance goal would depend on certain conditions, particularly the ambient air temperature and pressure and the cooling water temperature at the time of the test, and the quality of the fuel. And there were details of equipment settings, various measurements and such to be discussed and agreed upon.

We met in a dingy conference room at the plant, lined with shelves full of equipment manuals, regulatory rule binders and engineering drawings. Almost immediately upon sitting down, the manufacturer's senior engineer turned to the guaranteed heat rate section of the contract and pointed out that the calculation was based on an ideal, unrealistic assumption that there would be no exhaust gas leakage around the steam boiler sections. In fact, this leakage could amount to roughly a 3% loss of heat from the system, posing a significant reduction in power generation and fuel efficiency. He then suggested that we could not use the guaranteed heat rate as a standard upon which to base the performance test, but that we do a new calculation, which would result in a lower performance target.

It seemed to me that this proposed change represented a classic bait-and-switch tactic by the manufacturer. Astounded, I watched the discussion unfold. As a consultant, I felt very uncomfortable about attempting to intervene in this discussion, which was really about contractual terms, and not just technical details.

The utility engineers, clearly in over their heads, immediately agreed that the manufacturer's engineer was technically correct, and that the performance test should not reference the guaranteed heat rate, but a new calculation instead. Frozen in my seat by what I was witnessing, with no attorney or contract administrator in the room, I watched the engineers give an enormous financial gift to the manufacturer without any objection or attempt at business negotiation.

I felt that my best policy was to observe and report all this to the management staff later, because there would be time to take corrective action if needed. I checked this decision with my manager back at EPRI as well, just to confirm my judgment. When I subsequently reported what had occurred to the plant superintendent and engineering manager, they decided to let the engineers' decision stand, rather that complicate the situation.

I resolved that in my own work, I would always think of every meeting as a business meeting, because no matter the subject, there would be business implications. Sometimes the relationship to business factors can seem remote, but they are there. And the astute person will recognize when a discussion has reached beyond the purview of a particular specialty, such as engineering.

This mode of thinking came to permeate my leadership methods, and I developed a penchant for teaching my employees about the business, so that they would be able to reach better judgments in their everyday work. This approach paid off handsomely over the long run for the organizations that I ran and, I believe, for the employees who learned those lessons well.

Product Development and the Customer

Just where does the customer fit into the product development process? Most commercial companies these days have rather robust marketing and R&D organizations that understand how to define customer requirements and preferences fairly accurately. That's been true in many areas of consumer products for a very long time.

It hasn't always been that way in all industries. I learned something of the chasm that existed between product developers and users in the electric utility industry of the 1970s. I have three stories to share from that part of my career to illuminate the depth and breadth of that chasm.

The first story is about R&D in MHD electric power generation, which is based on the idea of accelerating an electrically conductive fluid (liquid or gas) through something that looks like a rocket nozzle lined with electrodes to capture electrical current. The nozzle is situated in the field of a powerful magnet, and the motion of the conductive fluid through the magnetic field creates electrical voltage across the nozzle, which can be tapped to produce electrical current. The idea is to be able to use fluids that are much higher in temperature than steam, in order to generate electricity more efficiently than with conventional methods. That's enough of the theory for the purpose of this story.

Many researchers in many nations have been engaged in research in MHD power generation over decades, for both commercial and military purposes. When I became a project manager at EPRI in 1973, MHD became one of my areas of responsibility.

There was an article of faith that seemed to permeate the US MHD research community at that time, which was that a successful commercial MHD power generation system would have to demonstrate at least 50% thermal efficiency (conversion of fuel energy into electricity) as compared with conventional systems that could do a bit above 40%, and that this was an achievable goal. As best I could figure, this was a political objective, designed to entice Congressional funding of the research efforts.

This objective translated into a number of intense laboratory projects to identify electrode materials that could stand up to the corrosive gases and slag produced by coal combustion. By the time I became involved, many years had been spent in this effort, without true success. However, a number of materials had been found that could stand up to somewhat lower combustion temperatures that would yield thermal efficiencies in the mid-forties. I saw this as an interesting result that deserved focused evaluation.

I created a set of projects to develop conceptual designs of coal-fired MHD power plants based on these laboratory results and projected efficiencies. The results indicated that such a plant could compete economically with conventional plants.

My supervisor, Mr. Al Dolbec, and I did our own historical research into the way that new power generation technologies had entered the utility market, and we found that uniformly, they entered in forms that barely competed with existing technology. The idea was to get the technology into the market in the minimum viable form, and then let the market drive the development of the technology toward its ultimate capability. (Note the similarity to the Minimum Viable Product concept that HP adopted in the 1990s for its electronic products.)

Based on this investigation, and considering how it might apply to MHD, Al and I presented a technical paper at a prestigious power industry conference in 1980, and it was subsequently published by the Institute of Electrical and Electronic Engineers (IEEE)[4]. That paper won an award from the technical committee on power generation, no doubt with the support of like-minded friends in the US Department of Energy and the utility industry.

These ideas heavily influenced the Federal R&D program, and EPRI continued to lead in representing the needs of the utility industry in this effort.

So there's something to keep in mind when developing a leap in technology. It doesn't have to be the biggest possible leap the first time out. This is about mitigating implementation risk in the development, while understanding the trade-offs with market risk.

The other two stories are from later in my EPRI work, when I took on the problems of poor reliability with existing gas turbine power plants. These plants had generally been sold as units that could be sited remotely and then started up as desired by a dispatcher at a central facility, in order to meet daily peak demand for electricity within a geographical region. However, these units had a penchant for not starting when desired, or breaking down soon after starting up. This situation was viewed as a limiting factor in the potential for developing base-load combined cycle power plants fired by coal-derived liquid or gaseous fuels. At last, I was working on something with higher perceived priority among the myriad of technological developments that EPRI was pursuing.

I began working particularly with General Electric and Westinghouse on gas turbine reliability issues. Those two companies, plus Pratt & Whitney, accounted for most of the installed base of gas turbine power plants in the US at the time.

My second story about involving customers in product development comes from when General Electric was about to introduce their very first microprocessor-based control system for gas turbine plants. This new control system was supposed to fix a lot of reliability problems that utilities had experienced with the earlier electromechanical systems. GE had planned no commercial site testing before beginning sales of the new system for retrofits in existing plants and for new construction.

I suggested that they might want to try this out in an existing plant with a willing utility. I even lined up a plant in Arizona, which Arizona Power was happy to offer up for a test.

The GE project manager's response was, "There's nothing those people can teach us about these control systems." I took this to mean that the people in GE R&D assumed that they knew everything that had been experienced by the utilities with their old control systems, and that the utility people weren't smart enough to contribute to a new design. It was also clear that the GE folks were concerned that EPRI would play a sort-of "Good Housekeeping" role for evaluating new products, despite my assurances that the intent was, rather, to have the most successful product introduction possible, from the perspectives of all parties.

Eventually I cajoled the key GE personnel into a meeting at the utility. After a knowledgeable presentation of problems with the reliability, usability and maintainability of the existing control system by the plant staff and many questions about the new system, the GE people relented. The test proceeded and produced substantial lessons about the new equipment. As a result, GE made a variety of design changes to the control system before it was introduced to the market. And I think their people learned some valuable lessons about how to work with the market during product development.

My third story, relating to Westinghouse, is equally revealing of the times. My own interviews of gas turbine power plant personnel around the country indicated that fuel oil systems (pumps, pressure regulators, etc.) were quite often to blame for plant outages of Westinghouse units, as well as those of other manufacturers.

Westinghouse R&D had been pursuing its own internal analysis of reliability issues, but without any strong input from the field. So I went to work on them and was pleased when one particular combined-cycle plant manager, with Florida Power and Light, asked if he could meet with people from Westinghouse R&D about this. I was gratified to find that the Westinghouse people were enthused by the idea, and so the meeting was set.

The Westinghouse team members were eager to share their own analyses of reliability issues with their gas turbine plants. These studies were largely theoretical, based on Failure Modes and Effects Analysis (FMEA). FMEA is a well-established, systematic method of analyzing what can go wrong in a system and what the effects would be of each mode of failure. The method depends on many quantitative estimates of failure rates of components and subsystems, and of the probabilities of various adverse effects occurring in the wake of each kind of failure. Accurate identification of failure modes and effects and of the failure probabilities is critical to producing a realistic result. Otherwise, it's garbage in, garbage out.

The Westinghouse team had confidently concluded that a certain set of problems were most prevalent with their systems, but they had sought no access to actual plant data to confirm their conclusions. Our meeting was their first chance to test their analysis and conclusions against real-world experience. So this was really a test of their methodology.

When the Westinghouse team finished their presentation to a room full of plant engineers, maintenance technicians, shift supervisors and managers, the plant superintendent rose to speak.

"That's a very fine analysis," he said, "but those problems you predict as the most prevalent ones are not at all the problems that we have experienced at this plant." To corroborate his statement, he proceeded to present statistics of what had failed over the years at his plant. There was little correlation between Westinghouse's FMEA results and the real experience of this power plant staff. The Westinghouse folks were suitably humbled. The amazing thing to me is that they could have asked for that real-world input at the beginning of their project, instead of at the end.

This meeting eventually generated a project toward improvement of Westinghouse's fuel oil system design. A barrier had been broken.

It seemed to me that something was wrong systemically in the relationships between the R&D departments of GE and Westinghouse and their respective customers. The real-world data at the heart of the issues were not being accessed by the people who could fix the problems. I believed that the causes of this issue rested in competitive secrecy, some professional arrogance, and perhaps other factors on the part of the manufacturers, as well as some insularity and accumulated discouragement among their utility customers.

It's worth noting that the Federal Government had collected plant outage information for decades, but it lacked the data resolution to identify causes, because it was only intended to identify unplanned outage duration statistics for rate-making purposes. So the details were jettisoned in favor of just the figures on outage hours per year.

I believed that EPRI could break this cycle among the utilities and the manufacturers. I eventually initiated a project that involved a third-party consultant collecting raw maintenance tags, usually written by plant technicians, from about 27 power plants. The consultant analyzed the data and then passed the tags confidentially to the respective equipment manufacturers, which included GE, Westinghouse and Pratt & Whitney. A lot of hard negotiating and diplomatic persuasion went into getting this project started, and it paid off handsomely in enlightening the manufacturers and the utilities about what was really happening out in the field. I was happy with that project, and I understand that it continued for years after my departure from EPRI.

So my message to product developers is to be creative and courageous in including market sources in the analysis of market experience and customer requirements. Theoretical analyses and focus groups are great, but nothing beats actual, raw, objective data from the field. After all, once the product is sold, the customer is the first one to know when something breaks and what the circumstances were.

What Will You Do When It Breaks?

Back when I was a young buck at EPRI, I was very fortunate to be working with a number of much more senior project managers and members of the technical staff, who were more than willing to share their accumulated wisdom. I had developed great respect and affection for many of them. One of these, the late Mr. Seymour B. "Sy" Alpert, returned to the office one afternoon from a presentation by a researcher about a particular advanced power plant technology. Sharing the story with some of us, Sy admitted that he hadn't really understood the presentation. "I had no idea what he was talking about!" So at the end of the presentation, as he related, he had asked his favorite question: "What will you do if it doesn't work?" That question, as Sy said it often did, generated another presentation that proved more enlightening than the first one.

I always smile when I remember Sy's story and his favorite question. But since everything doesn't work eventually, I have often found it more effective to ask, "What will you do when it breaks?" That became my version of Sy's favorite question.

Not long after, I was riding in the brand new, luxurious automobile of Mr. Jerome "Jerry" Weiss, another of the more experienced staff members, who had also heard Sy's story. He was proudly demonstrating the vehicle, which was quite well-appointed and comfortable. This being the mid-1970s, it was powered by a diesel engine, and Jerry was very pleased that his fuel costs would be lower as a result.

We were on the way back from lunch, stopped at an intersection, when Jerry asked, "So what do you think of it?"

Well, I was listening to the idling engine make its characteristic, comical noise: *pocketa-pocketa-pocketa*. And being something of a wise guy, I couldn't help myself. I decided to put my own twist on Sy's favorite question.

"I just have one question, Jerry." He looked over at me. With a straight face, I asked, "How can you tell when it's broken?"

His answer came without an instant's hesitation. "Get out!" he yelled.

***

But now, let's fast-forward to late 1998, when I began a consultancy to TRW Space Systems in Redondo Beach, California. For the fourth time, I had been engaged to help a satellite manufacturer figure out how to improve satellite integration and test. Only this time, it was a military project, aiming to put a constellation of more than 30 satellites in orbit so as to constantly monitor the earth for ballistic missile launches and track their upper stages via their heat signatures. This was part of the "Star Wars" Strategic Defense Initiative concept of missile defense conceived during the Reagan Administration.

TRW had a long history of building one-off satellites, mostly of a scientific or military nature, and each of those projects generally took many years. Now the company was bidding to become prime contractor on a US Air Force contract to build more than 30 identical satellites, delivering one per month to the launch site on a strict schedule. This was a very different kind of manufacturing than they were used to, and they had engaged the HP consulting team to bring our manufacturing and test expertise into their bidding process. In the end, the strategy worked, as we taught them how to best design the flow of their factory, the test processes and utilization of information from test, as well as other factors that would be important to success.

My first meeting on the site, to discuss the potential consulting project, began with TRW's presentation about the satellite program and the planning that their team had already done. The presenter, Chuck, a jovial, cordial man in his fifties, worked for the director of satellite integration and test. He would become my primary contact to help coordinate the consulting project. Several other TRW and HP people were present.

At the conclusion of his presentation, Chuck proudly presented an animation of the anticipated factory flow. The animation showed various integration and test stations, with the satellites being built up gradually and tested, including final testing of the fully integrated satellites. In order to meet the production schedule, the factory would require several test stations operating in parallel for the full-up testing of the integrated satellites. The animation showed satellites moving smoothly through this imaginary factory. Chuck looked quite pleased with this vision of the future.

But there was no provision for anything going wrong in the testing. No provision for failures. I remembered Sy Alpert's favorite question.

"How many satellites has TRW produced that did not fail in integrated system test?" I began.

"None," came the expected answer from Chuck, along with a troubled look.

"So, what will you do when a satellite breaks?"

Silence. I didn't let it last. "When a satellite fails a system test, what will you do? Will you leave it attached to that test system, so that the failure can be properly diagnosed as to whether it is an actual failure of the satellite or rather a failure of the test system, or of the interface between them? Or will you move the satellite off the main production line to a diagnostic test station, where you'll have to start the testing over, and possibly not be able to replicate the failure? And when the problem's fixed, where will you retest the satellite?"

"Uh," Chuck stammered, "well, we really haven't thought about those questions."

"Either way, if a significant number of these satellites fail their functional tests at least once, you will need additional test stations, in order to keep shipments on schedule. It could easily be twice the number you're thinking. Those flow decisions, the design of the test stations and the effective use of test data will be critical."

The TRW people were sobered by these thoughts. Their nice, animated factory model, and perhaps their whole cost model for the program, had just gone out the window.

"We need you here," Chuck concluded.

So much better than, "Get out!" I thought. *And thanks again, Sy.*

Learning and improvement come from failure, much more than from success. In a factory, understanding how things vary from ideal, how you'll know, and what you'll do about it is the key to effectiveness.

Lastly, it's not just important to know what you'll do when something breaks. It's just as important to know how to tell whether things are getting better when you introduce changes.

A Systems Engineering Analogy

Systems engineers understand that opportunities for system performance improvements often come from improving the performance of the interfaces between system elements, even more so than from improving the performance of individual system elements.

It's worth noting, in this light, that the changes that I eventually recommended to TRW consisted only partly of improvements to individual pieces of equipment, processes or departments, but equally to the interfaces between departments. In presenting my recommendations, one of the charts that I drew for TRW's management team was a simple bubble chart of their organizational structure, emphasizing the interfaces between the major organizational departments. And I asked them the question, "If

TRW makes the changes that we've recommended here, how will the company measure the effects?"

I might just as well have asked, "How will you know it's working right?" And that's not so much different from asking Sy's favorite question.

They needed to answer that question in order to effectively manage the significant changes that were contemplated. The answer would begin with designing the flow of process and cost data among the departments so as to rapidly signal change. That data would need to be converted effectively into information useful for decision-making. That's the essence of managing change in an organization.

Having looked across the boundary from product development to other areas, it is time to look at manufacturing itself.

World Class Manufacturing and Beyond

After several years leading a production engineering team in a product division of HP, I accepted an offer to move to the Microwave Technology Division, in order to lead two small manufacturing product lines. This division produced components used mainly in products made by other HP divisions.

One of my new teams was the magnetics group. This was a group with a very long history, because it manufactured the specialized magnetic crystalline spheres that were the heart of every microwave resonator and filter in HP's broad line of microwave test and measurement instruments. These high-precision components generated or detected the microwave signals for the instruments, and they had to do those jobs perfectly, in order for the rest of each instrument to operate properly. These crystals were critical to products that represented sales revenues of about $1 billion per year at the time.

Despite this importance, the group had been allowed to drift without close management attention for quite a long time. It had a reputation for poor product quality and delivery, increasing pricing, and very slow development of new products needed by the customer divisions. My assignment resulted from management's recognition that this situation needed to be turned around. Despite the group's small size, I felt that it was an important responsibility.

I soon learned that engineering investment in the technology and support for the group had been minimized for years, and that a great deal of process "creep" had insinuated itself into the production processes. The processes for growing crystal were not as originally defined, and those for manufacturing spheres from the crystal were never fully developed with a comprehensive engineering theory.

My other important observation was that the team's morale was abysmal. The supervisor of the production operators, although sincere and making a great effort, demonstrated poor skill in the performance of his duties, and this had not been addressed by higher management until my assignment. The team had a reputation for petty bickering and whining about things incidental to the business. They didn't seem to have any interest in the business itself.

Managing Your Boss

I chose to coach the supervisor intensively to see how he would respond. I also coached his team of production operators directly. One day early on, I had a "communication lunch" with the production operators. One of the things they told me was that they had repeatedly requested new lockers for their personal belongings over several months, but the supervisor had not responded. While keeping in mind that there was a performance issue, I decided to give the team a bit of power, hoping that it would lead them to take more responsibility for improvement of their area.

"Did you ever hear of the idea of managing your boss?" I asked the six people gathered around the table.

One of the operators replied, "No, but it sounds great! What do you mean?"

"You know, your supervisor is very busy, and I'm sure that he hasn't forgotten your request, but it takes time to do the research on which lockers to buy and where to find them, and to prepare the purchase request. What if you all did that research, picked the lockers you want, gave him that information with a bit of justification, and filled out the purchase requisition yourselves? Then all he would have to do is sign the requisition and submit it to me. I would approve it in a second."

"That would be great! We already know which ones we want." There were smiles all around the table. They suddenly understood that they could do much to solve their own problems and not be a victim of someone else's workload.

The supervisor was pleased with the new initiative of the team and relieved to have that item off his to-do list. The team had its new lockers shortly afterward. I followed up, of course, with some coaching for the supervisor, in delegating tasks and teaching his employees.

Such was my first little success in empowering the manufacturing employees.

At Last, Someone Cares

In a process that had been developed about 25 years earlier, the crystals were grown in a furnace from mixtures of various metallic oxide powders. It was a hazardous process because of the toxic nature of some of the powders and the high temperature of the furnace. Only one man knew and performed that process. A billion dollars in annual sales depended on his practical knowledge, but he was thinking of quitting HP to pursue an outside business interest.

Likewise, only one woman performed the mixing of the powders in platinum crucibles for insertion into the furnace. Without engineering guidance, the mixing procedure had degraded over the years.

Making these jobs more attractive, adding engineering guidance, and getting some additional operators trained on these processes were immediate priorities for me.

The mixing equipment and the furnace were located in a dingy basement area, far from the attractive factory upstairs, where tiny cubes sawn from the crystals were ground into precision spheres, magnetically tested and aligned, and glued to ceramic rods for eventual insertion into microwave circuits. The concrete walls of the crystal growth area were unpainted, and the area exhibited twenty-five years' accumulated dust in nooks and crannies. No wonder no one wanted to work there.

A short while into this assignment, I became concerned that members of the team, over 25 years, might have been exposed to potentially toxic heavy metals. I insisted that we have appropriate medical tests performed on everyone associated with the production operation, even including former employees, and to continue with ongoing health monitoring for the current team. The manufacturing management team agreed, as I would have expected in HP, and the testing was carried out. I was pleased to learn that no one was found to have evidence of such poisoning.

Simultaneously, I proposed to management that we do a complete clean-up of the basement area, including thorough painting in white, new lighting, some updated equipment, and new procedures for maintaining cleanliness. Again, despite a hefty cost, management agreed. We implemented these changes rather quickly, and the results were very satisfactory.

Our initial actions of medical testing and the clean-up of the crystal growth area accomplished more than the visible results of a cleaner, more controllable process and increased confidence in the health and safety of our employees. They also raised the team's morale and confidence in management. These initiatives had been the first steps taken in decades to improve the work environment, and the team members gained new trust that I had the power to make things better for them. More than that, it showed that someone cared about them, finally.

The clean-up was actually part of a much broader improvement effort that was proposed by our production engineer, Larry Pendergrass, whose education was actually in applied physics, an excellent match to the needs of this operation. (Larry eventually would move on to become a technology executive in his own right.) Larry had broad rein to drive the improvement of all the production processes in the area, and he addressed these in a logical sequence, from crystal growth through sphere fabrication and test. His analysis showed that we would not be able to achieve process control without first revamping the crystal growth process, and that a general clean-up of the area and the process itself was a necessary first step. So the clean-up had two objectives: personnel health and safety, and production process control.

As these changes were proceeding, I asked for one or two volunteers from the group to learn the crystal growth process. Some days later, two of the women in the group came to my cubicle (no one had formal offices in our division) and asked if they could speak with me. I set aside my paperwork and invited them to sit at my little conference table. One of them asked, with a bit of trepidation, "If we refuse to learn the crystal growth process, will we be fired?"

Without hesitation, I replied. "Of course not. You weren't hired with that expectation, and I don't think it would be fair to make that a consequence now. I understand that the process is a bit frightening, but I'm determined to make improvements to the equipment that will make it as safe as possible. I'm hoping that we'll have volunteers from the group, but if not, I'll figure out how to hire someone to take on that responsibility."

The same woman asked, "If someone volunteers, will they be paid more?"

"Well, I would hope that increased knowledge and acceptance of increased responsibility would be reflected in that person's performance ranking and, in turn, in their rate of pay over time.

"How soon do you want this to happen?"

"The sooner the better. A lot of our customer divisions' revenues depend on us producing these crystals. I don't think we ought to wait around for something bad to happen."

The two women looked at each other and murmured a few words back and forth.

"We'll do it."

Another step forward. And I was glad it was the women, because it meant that we would have to modify the equipment to accommodate their smaller physical stature, and that would further ensure safety overall.

I shook hands with each of them. "Thank you for your courage in stepping up. I really appreciate it."

Eliminating Variability is the First Step to Quality

As explained to me by the inventor of our processes for producing the crystal and spheres, the original crystal growth process had been designed to produce a broad distribution of electromagnetic properties in each crystal, so that spheres could be produced and selected from each growth to match the specifications of various customers. This approach was intended to minimize the number of crystal growths required each year and seemed good enough to meet the customers' technical performance requirements at the time.

However, the net result was also a broad distribution in the quality of the spheres produced from each crystal. Some spheres had inclusions of unwanted metal particles, the way a diamond might show the flaw of an inclusion. Others had crystal dislocation planes in them, or other defects. As the customers' requirements evolved and tightened over the years, the old crystal growth process had been rendered ever more inadequate. The crystal defects impacted the performance of the spheres in the microwave circuits, made our customer's circuit alignment processes more complicated and diminished the ultimate performance of their products. In other words, our own process variability caused further variability in our customers' processes as well, thereby decreasing quality and raising costs throughout the production system.

Larry Pendergrass proposed that we would be better off if we tried growing crystal with a very tight distribution of electromagnetic properties, targeting each crystal growth toward a particular customer's specification. We agreed to try this approach. The results were a textbook tale of quality improvement.

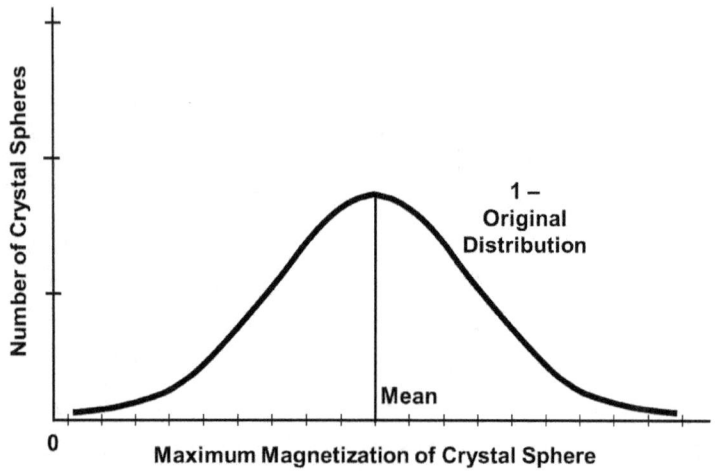

Figure 1
Illustration of distribution of product parameter.
A broad distribution of a particular parameter in units produced by a production process. Here, the parameter was a particular magnetic property of crystal spheres.

Suppose you are producing some product and achieving a very broad distribution of results. That distribution might look something like the graph of line 1 in Figure 1. I've chosen the well-known Gaussian distribution that represents many natural processes, and I'm calling this curve "Maximum Magnetization" so as to loosely represent one of the performance parameters we were working on. The height of the curve at any point along the horizontal axis represents the number of spheres with that value. (This is a simplification, of course, because in reality, the spheres were grouped in small increments of maximum magnetization.) And the total area under the curve represents the total number of spheres made from a crystal growth. In fact, this curve is not a bad representation of the distribution we were seeing from each crystal growth. The "mean" value was approximately at the center of the distribution, and we were able to pick spheres for various customers from all over this distribution.

What we wanted to do was to tighten this distribution in each crystal growth, so that we could design a particular growth for a particular customer. Now, let's suppose that we selected a customer with a target maximum magnetic strength equal to the mean of the distribution. The customer specification would allow a range of values on either side of the mean, as represented by the dashed lines in Figure 2.

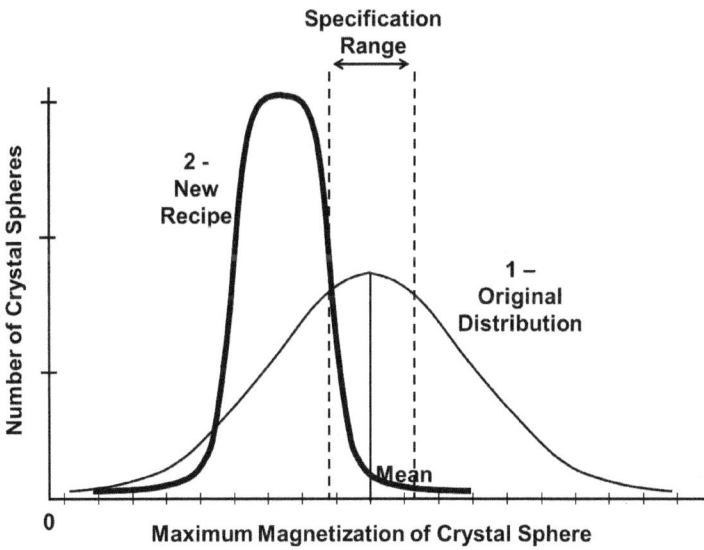

Figure 2
Our first try at tightening the distribution.
We achieved a tight distribution, as represented by line 2, but not centered on the target value within the product's specification range.

We grew a new crystal, having adjusted the metallic powder mix to try to center the distribution at the center of the customer specification. Our revised process was intended to provide a very tight distribution around that value. Unfortunately, with our limited understanding of how the process would react to our changes in the mix "recipe" for the metallic powders and in the crystal growth conditions, we missed on the first try, creating a distribution represented by line 2 in Figure 2.

Looking at that curve, one can see that only a small fraction of the spheres fell within the specification range. A nearly complete miss. However, we didn't look at this as a failure, but rather as a step in learning. We were gratified to see the tight distribution of values that we'd been hoping for. We were confident that we'd be able to adjust the recipe to move the mean of our new, tight distribution to where we wanted it.

We achieved that result on our next try, as illustrated by line 3 in Figure 3. And it was good-quality crystal, uniform throughout, so we got a tremendously high yield of spheres from that batch. Suddenly, we had an enormous supply of product for that particular customer. Since this represented the largest order volume of all our sphere products, we were hopeful that the days of late shipments would be behind us.

We sent sphere samples from this crystal growth to the customer, and they responded that these were the best-performing spheres they had seen. The uniformity of the crystal yielded not only a tight distribution of maximum magnetization, but of other performance parameters as well. The customers' circuit alignment processes had gone more smoothly and more quickly than ever. They wanted to know what had happened, so Larry explained the process changes. The customer readily agreed to accept the changes, with great compliments on our initiative.

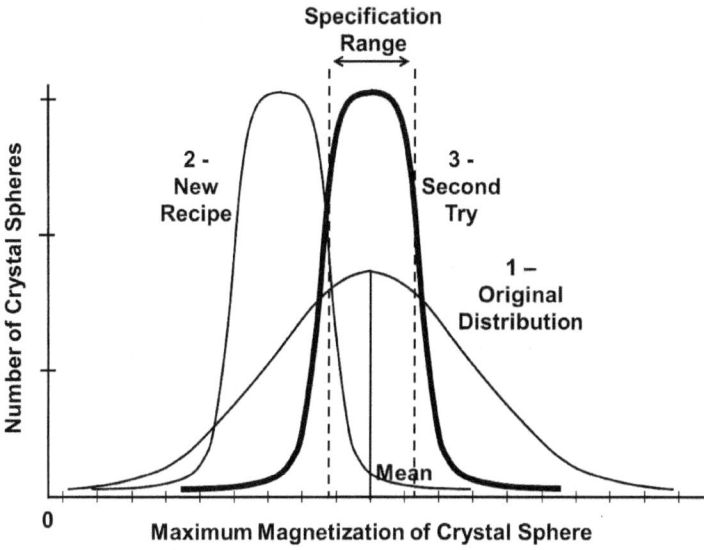

Figure 3
Hitting the target.
After adjusting the crystal mix recipe, we maintained the same tight distribution but shifted its mean value so that the distribution was centered in the specification range, as represented by line 3. Most of the resulting products met the specification.

We subsequently made similar changes for our other products, producing a crystal batch for each one. Uniformly, the customers raved about the quality of the new product. We knew that we had moved into a new regime of higher quality, which spurred the team on to more improvement projects. We never looked back.

The improvement steps we had followed are, in fact, a good general approach to achieving high yield of product when starting with low yield. First, understand the distribution. Next, understand how to tighten the distribution, that is, to *minimize the variability* of the product, unit to unit. Finally, understand how to move the mean of the distribution into the center of the desired range. If one starts the other way, by trying to move the mean of a broad distribution, there will be little improvement to show for it, and perhaps no direct path to tightening the distribution.

Considering the concept of "product" broadly, it is valuable to understand that this approach would be true for any process, even administrative processes. Minimizing variability is the starting place for quality improvement in any process.

One aspect of variability that showed up in this operation, and others that I ran subsequently, had to do with spontaneous experimentation. Engineers and production operators would undertake to make process improvements on product that was then shipped to customers, with little or no management involvement or customer notification. I put my foot down, gently. What I told these teams is that they could do all the experimentation that time and money allowed, but not on products that were to be shipped to customers. Instead, when a process change was deemed production-worthy, then we would implement that change in a controlled fashion, including appropriate trials by customers.

These lessons about variability are nicely addressed within the well-developed, data-driven improvement cycle called "Define, Measure, Analyze, Improve and Control" (DMAIC)[5]:

- Define the problem, improvement activity, opportunity for improvement, project goals, and customer (internal and external) requirements.
- Measure process performance.
- Analyze the process to determine root causes of variation and poor performance (defects).
- Improve process performance by addressing and eliminating the root causes.
- Control the improved process and future process performance.

This methodology provides a well-defined framework for improving, optimizing and stabilizing business processes and technical designs. Six Sigma methodology employs the DMAIC framework.

Developing the Team so They No Longer Needed Me

Gradually, we continued to make further improvements. One of these was in the area of "process ownership." At the time I came aboard, the entire division operated on the basis that the manufacturing engineers "owned" the manufacturing processes, in that they were responsible for investigating all process variations and anomalies and for all decisions regarding the processes and equipment. As a result, the engineers spent almost all of their time "firefighting," responding to crises, with virtually no time left to work on advancing the technologies. The production operators were not empowered to make decisions, but had to operate the processes according to orders from the engineers.

Generally speaking, the engineers in the division were frustrated with the way things worked. They suffered tremendous stress from the constant firefighting and the lack of professional fulfillment that this environment imposed. Meanwhile, a similar frustration was reflected among the production operators, who felt that problems weren't being solved fast enough, because the availability of engineering support was limited. Operators also felt that they could contribute more, if they were allowed to. Most of them were eager to learn.

I saw that we had the opportunity to liberate these people from the forced adherence to old ways that had prevailed before my arrival. Within the groups that I led, we gradually transitioned to a way of working in which the production operators "owned" their processes, accepting responsibility for quality, schedule, and all other factors, while the engineers became their consultants and advisors.

The key to making this change was intensive education of the operators in the theory of their processes, the methods of statistical process control, and how to recognize when a process wasn't working as designed or when it had exceeded the limits of the operators' own knowledge. We began this educational process early on, and the formal change in process ownership did not happen until that knowledge was in hand. As a result, the transition was generally smooth, without process upset, and we witnessed rapid gains in process yields, product quality, on-time delivery and other metrics. The satisfaction levels of the operators and engineering staff rose dramatically and rapidly. And my job got easier.

I was pleased that this new regime of process ownership gradually became the norm across the division.

Throughout the team's improvement efforts, I focused consistently on a few outcome metrics, three of which were customer-facing, namely, our on-time delivery rate, the rate of customer rejections of our products, and the new product introduction lead time; and three of which were internal: production yield, production cycle time, and costs. That combination of external and internal metrics provided an effective balance of customer focus and attention to the details of our processes. I made the results visible to everyone on the team and discussed them consistently in meetings. The team became focused on those results with me, and on the changes that we needed to make to improve them.

Over a period of about a year, our team's performance improved dramatically, and customers began complimenting us regularly. Whining and bickering among the team were long gone. The focus was on problem-solving and improvement.

One day I was talking with the production operator who used to be the sole grower of our crystals. He was contributing a great deal to several of our improvement projects, and we had just finished discussing one of them. "Tell me," I asked, "Are you still thinking of leaving the company?

"Not really," he said. "This is like reading a good book, and I kinda want to see how it ends."

More than that, he had become one of the authors writing that ending. As the Tin Man might say, win your employee's heart, and you gain the power of his brain. And in the bargain, I would say, also the skill of his hands and, perhaps, his courage.

The next steps in developing this team happened rapidly. Building on the idea of "managing your boss," I realized that I was working too hard on annual capital budgeting. I was working with the engineers and the production supervisor to understand what equipment improvements would help us, and how much each of those would help financially. The team made estimates of the cost of each equipment improvement, and I would then make decisions on these investment priorities, rejecting some and keeping others, and then put together a capital budget proposal for my boss.

What I realized is that I was in the way. There was no reason that I could not educate the engineers and the supervisor about capital budgeting. So I did that, showing them how to make the financial trade-offs that led to decisions on what to invest in, and what not to, and how to set priorities among the projects to be done. Gradually, they took over the annual capital budgeting process, defining the technical issues, investigating and deciding on potential solutions, developing cost estimates, and doing economic trade-off studies. They would compile the proposal, review it with me, and I would pass it along to my manager.

As a result, I had less to do, they learned more about the business, and all the homework to prepare for purchase orders was done along the way. Upon approval of the budget, they would prepare the purchase orders on the project schedule that they had defined. My part of this task became easy. I had helped them figure out how to manage their boss, and I loved it.

I even taught them my trick of planning what they would do if my boss directed a 10% cut in our capital budget and, contrarily, if 10% more money became available at some point in the fiscal year. The latter almost always happened, because other groups weren't as prepared as we were to spend their budgets, so money would always become available to us later in the year. I developed a reputation among the management team for always managing my capital budget well and always being prepared for changes. It was a joy to give my team the credit.

These changes in the capital budgeting and implementation processes had one more benefit that's worth mentioning. Since the team members shared in analyzing, preparing and implementing the budget, purchasing the equipment, and integrating that equipment into the operations, each member was heavily invested personally in the success of all that, and in the success of the team effort. This added to the cohesion and strength of the team as well as its members. From my view, it was a fine bit of organizational systems engineering that was remarkably easy to figure out and implement.

As I taught the team more and more about our business, I found that they were eager to take on more of the responsibility for the processes and the results. Gradually, I found that I was becoming an advisor and consultant to them. I was able to step back and consider the bigger picture of our business, our customers, and the team's development. I felt that I was continually gaining the higher ground and the greater perspective. My mantra became, *"Give up control to get control."* And I had more free time to practice Management by Walking Around (a topic we'll address presently) and for an occasional afternoon round of golf. Management heaven! It was time to take on something else.

Starting a Bigger Turn-Around

Fortunately for me, my manager had similar plans. He asked me to take on half of our much larger operation that produced microwave thin film circuits. These were miniature circuit boards, consisting of ceramic or crystal bases with various components and electrical traces on them. Seeing any of their physical details required a microscope.

These circuits were made via chemical vapor deposition and other processes in a clean-room fabrication area, "the fab," where everyone wore "bunny suits" – white coats, head and foot coverings, and gloves. Multiple, identical circuits were formed on each ceramic substrate. When that was done, the substrates left the clean room and entered my new domain, "separation and test," where they were sawn into individual circuits, those circuits were tested, adjusted if necessary, subjected to wire-bonding and other processes, packaged and shipped to customers.

Until 1992, when I accepted this new assignment, the thin film manufacturing operation had been run by the time-honored process of "trickle-down" manufacturing, meaning that material was stuffed into the front end of the process, with the expectation that something would eventually trickle out the back end and into the waiting hands of the customer. It didn't work well.

On-time delivery was nearly non-existent. Quality was abysmal, and the number of quality problems seemed overwhelming. New products were stuck in a constipated development process for years. Costs were out of control.

Team morale was awful. Shortly after joining the group, I had to swiftly and decisively resolve an incident in which animosity over work-related disagreements had led one employee to threaten another with death. I hadn't experienced anything like this since being in the midst of violent trade union confrontations at a power plant in the 1970s, but that's another story.

A new manager for the fab, Roger Wylie, was assigned at the same time that I took over separation and test. He was another engineer by education, and a very good one.

Our boss sat us both down right after announcing our assignments and told us that our job was to cut production costs quickly, or see the department go out of business. He was right, too.

Roger and I got along very well, which was necessary if we were going to tame this tiger. We spent a lot of time getting to know each other and discussing the issues at hand.

One afternoon, Roger and I took a couple of flipchart stands and a bunch of felt pens to my house, sat down with a few beers, and started listing and diagramming the issues facing us. At first, it seemed almost overwhelming. But after some time, we recognized the common theme that, for every issue, process variability was the enemy. Variability was prevalent in our product development processes, in our production processes, in the way material flow was managed, in the way we processed engineering change orders, in the way we defined jobs and hired employees, and in the way we reported results. Everything that happened in our department was a process with rampant variability.

We declared war on variability. That was our starting point. We set priorities on what areas to attack, what each objective would be, and how we would delegate the tasks necessary to improvement in each area. We planned how to communicate these ideas and how to set up the team for success. As we finished our last beers, we toasted to our plan.

Work-in-Process Inventory is an Enemy of Quality

The thin film circuit department produced hundreds of different circuit products, identified by part numbers. The separation and test portion that reported to me was clogged with work-in-process (WIP) inventory, which means products that aren't finished being manufactured. There were mountains of WIP, all stored in transparent plastic desiccator boxes, protected from moisture and contaminants. Every workstation had stacks of desiccators. If we had waved a magic wand and completed all these products immediately, they would have sustained most of our customers for a year or more.

WIP inventory is a financial asset. It has value. At each step of the production process, a particular product has a particular value representing the cost of producing it up to that point. But in my mind, WIP represents a source of concern, because some of that value is at risk. It's at risk because the partially complete product might be defective, or it might become damaged, or it might be subject to customer design changes or order changes that would render it obsolete. In our trickle-down factory, it also represented a kind of psychological burden to the production team. WIP was there at the beginning of every shift, and it was still there at the end. From my view, it seemed as if we were trying to move a mountain with a teaspoon.

Most importantly, WIP inventory is also a kind of camouflage. It hides quality problems. If a test operator takes a part from WIP, tests it, and finds a defect, that defect might stem from a faulty process step that occurred months before. That makes problem-solving difficult and late. So WIP costs money as it sits there, aging. WIP is an enemy of quality.

At the time, it was common in the quality profession to liken production flow to a river. It's not a perfect analogy, because a river can overflow its banks. Flow in a water pipe or traffic on a freeway, where the flow really is constrained, might be better analogies.[6] But a river is a nice image and a reasonable starting place. In this analogy, the amount of material flowing through the factory is like the amount of water flowing down a river. Submerged rocks, representing quality problems and other impediments, slow the water flow. If you lower the river, you expose the rocks and make them visible. So, the analogy goes, if you lower the amount of WIP, you will expose the quality issues that slow the flow, so they can be remedied. That part is true, despite the limitations of the analogy.

Roger and I knew that we were not going to be able to make quick progress on the myriad quality problems we had until we had largely eliminated the massive WIP inventory.

Meanwhile, reviewing our finished-goods inventory, I found that we had plenty of finished inventory of many of our low-volume part numbers. But there were many high-volume part numbers for which we had little inventory in stock. This boded ill for our customers if we ran into serious quality problems with those parts. And it turned out that we already had serious quality problems with many of them. A lot of the WIP inventory represented our effort to catch up and get ahead on these problems.

So, our river was clogged with rocks that we couldn't see, and we kept dumping more and more water into the river in the effort to get some of it to trickle into the ocean, as it were. The more we dumped in, the bigger our quality issues became, so the river flow only became more impeded by bigger rocks. Making significant progress on quality was hopeless unless we changed something.

While all this thinking was going on, I had the good fortune to read Eliyahu M. Goldratt's *The Goal*,[7] which is structured as a novel about a manufacturing manager who is wrestling the kinds of problems that Roger and I were. It's brilliant. The hero is under so much stress at work that it's adversely affecting his home life, until he has an epiphany about how to solve the problems in the factory. I realized that I was living his life. I didn't just read the book, I devoured it, and I bought copies for Roger and several other people in the organization. It became an important touchstone for us all, but for none more than me, I think.

Roger and I made a fateful decision. We ordered all lot starts – all new batches of products – stopped until we had lowered the WIP inventory sufficiently to expose the rocks. That decision frightened many people. It frightened the accountants, who would see it as a sudden drop in the financial assets of the division. Their concern was echoed by our managers. It frightened our production supervisors, who could not foresee how this would affect workload on their teams. And the engineers were concerned about the rate at which quality issues would be exposed and, perhaps, raised to the level of crises.

Roger and I stuck to our guns. As WIP was gradually completed, the desiccators began to show some empty space. As the WIP dropped further and further over a few months, the quality problems made themselves clear at a reasonable rate that our people could handle. We assigned a team to each problem, and they attacked those problems with discipline and creativity. Gradually, the problems were resolved.

As the problems diminished, the material moved more quickly through the factory. The river was being cleared. As that happened, the WIP inventory dropped even more quickly. Average production lead time through the factory (the average time to complete a product lot from start to finish) dropped from months to weeks.

Despite a tremendous amount of communication from Roger and me, there were still concerns and some fear. One day, I was walking through the separation area, as I did at least daily. I stopped to chat with one of the production operators, and he seemed a bit hesitant. Finally, he said, "Paul, the desiccators are getting emptier. Are we going out of business?"

The question rather surprised me, since this operator and his peers had been through extensive communications and training related to the change. Yet, I understood that fear of a changing environment can be powerful even in the face of knowledge. This man was looking for some reassurance in the midst of a difficult voyage.

"Absolutely not," I said. "We're going to keep producing the same amount of product that we always have. It's just that we're removing obstacles in the way of finishing it quickly."

He did seem somewhat relieved.

As these improvements occurred, and we began transferring excess people to other departments, Roger and I resolved to maintain our headcount about 15% above the number necessary for production. This meant that the people had about 6 hours per week available to devote to training and development, as well as improvement projects. We retained that as our policy for the long term, and the team's continuous productivity improvement made this possible, even as we continued to shrink the size of the group.

Eventually, watching finished goods and WIP inventory closely, Roger and I turned on the spigot of production lot starts, part number by part number. By then, the desiccators in the separation and test area, as well as in the fab, were mostly empty.

At the same time, we changed to a Kanban system for controlling WIP. Kanban is a form of production control in which each station is allowed to send WIP to the next station only when the receiving station is ready to take more. More broadly, Kanban is one of a class of production control systems called "demand-pull." Each station effectively pulls material from the previous station when it's good and ready to do so. The Kanban approach sets rules for having just a few lots in queue for each station. That gives a bit more flexibility than having completely empty queues (desiccators, in our case). Our Kanban queues were designed so that each workstation would have several hours' or a shift's worth of work in the queue at the beginning of each shift.

Looking back, Roger and I hadn't just dropped all these new ideas on the production team. We had educated them all along. The first lesson was simply to say that we were embarking on a journey out of business necessity. We could not stay where we were. Cutting costs would mean fewer jobs in the immediate future, and those team members who chose to join us in the journey and help complete it would keep their jobs. Likewise, as the journey proceeded and jobs were eliminated, we would help the displaced people find new positions. No one was compelled to join us. If anyone didn't like the idea of that journey, we would be happy to help them find a position in another department, or even outside the company. No one flinched. As things progressed, by the way, we made good on our word about helping people find new positions. This was one of the things that won us the confidence and loyalty of the team.

We had asked everyone in the department to read Richard J. Schonberger's *World Class Manufacturing*,[8] a fine textbook on achieving the fundamental steps toward what's now called "lean manufacturing." Many of them also read *The Goal*. We had created a class that was a paper simulation of the production area, which we ran repeatedly for small groups of team members. Each person represented a workstation, and slips of paper were passed from one to the next, each representing a production lot. We first demonstrated the trickle-down approach to production control, and what resulted was a flood of paper representing WIP. Then we demonstrated a demand-pull system, and the result was a simulation of neat and quick production. People had grasped it right away.

So, as our journey proceeded, what we were doing was no surprise to anyone. But still, living it was different from simulating it.

A few months after we implemented the Kanban system, I was chatting with the same production operator who had earlier expressed concern for our jobs. I asked him how he felt about the change, in retrospect.

He beamed. "Paul, it's great! I used to go home feeling that I'd accomplished nothing. The desiccators were just as full at the end of shift as they were at the beginning. It was really depressing. Now, I come in, I look at the desiccator, I know what I'm supposed to get done, and at the end of shift, I've done my part, and I go home feeling like I accomplished something. I wouldn't go back to the old way for anything!"

There was a broader implication that I noticed among the production operators, as a result of the change in the production control system. It wasn't just that the individual operators felt more accomplished on their own. It was also the case that they felt that they were better supporting each other. In fulfilling the day's work, each operator was also fulfilling the needs of the operators working in the upstream and downstream operations, and that was an additional source of individual satisfaction. They had become more tuned into each other's needs and concerns about the processes, as well as each other's enthusiasm. Closer teamwork became an almost automatic side effect. The Tin Man and the Cowardly Lion were at work right alongside the Scarecrow.

Outsourcing and Automation

Along the way, we found several areas in which the team continually struggled. One of these was in the maintenance of certain exotic pieces of equipment. Our maintenance team was continually challenged by the problems of these systems, with the result that we suffered line shutdowns occasionally. Those shutdowns didn't show up on management radar when we had a river full of rocks in the form of WIP inventory, but when that was gone and we were running a demand-pull environment, every equipment outage was immediately visible.

After an assessment of the situation, the maintenance team recommended that we outsource maintenance on those pieces of equipment. After all, there were experts available outside our organization. So that's what we did, and those problems disappeared.

I think that some of the waves of outsourcing that have been done by industry were excuses for not finding ways to improve processes internally, when that could have been done instead. It is certainly worth understanding what the organization's core competencies are and must be, and what activities are not core to the business. The core competencies will generally be the things that fundamentally differentiate the organization from competitors, for example, or those that are absolutely critical to the company's mission and cannot be risked in the hands of outsiders. Non-core competencies are certainly potential candidates for outsourcing, but this does not mean that every non-core competency must be outsourced. In my view, the leadership and the team ought to do every reasonable thing they can to improve, with a particular eye on minimizing average actual production cycle time, as we'll discuss presently. When that's been done, and analyses of return on investment and of further cycle time reduction opportunities support outsourcing, then it's entirely appropriate. Outsourcing shouldn't be a goal, but just a tool.

Making a decision to outsource may be painful. I have unpleasant memories of proposing and leading the outsourcing of a technology that had been invented many years before by people in my own HP division. Competent external competitors had arisen, leading to erosion of our previous advantages in selling to internal customers, despite some amount of technological lead that we maintained. A great deal of analysis and exploration revealed that outsourcing was clearly the best business decision available to us, and it was best for our customers as well. When I proposed this solution and the reasons, I encountered a stunning amount of opposition and anger among my colleagues. We proceeded with the outsourcing effort eventually. In the end, the project was very successful in all respects, but I learned some harsh lessons about how difficult and even thankless such an effort can be.

This project occurred while we were simultaneously working to save our magnetics group, as I described above. The magnetics technology, while troublesome, was critical to HP's huge business in test and measurement instrumentation. It could not be relegated to outside suppliers without entailing unacceptable risks. It was a core competence that had been allowed to deteriorate, and we simply had to recover it. So we saved one operation while outsourcing another.

Such decisions about what is a core competence and what is not, and what ought to be outsourced and what shouldn't, are some of the most important operational decisions that business leaders must make. My own experience suggests that nothing should be taken for granted in this process, and that everything should be subjected to the most sober analysis and planning, including even the potential emotional reactions of stakeholders.

I think of automation in a similar vein. There are some processes that are not amenable to tight process control when in the hands of humans. A spacecraft during launch simply has to have onboard computers to handle the millisecond response times required to maintain control. In a factory, there often are fabrication or alignment processes that are best performed by machines, in the interests of quality and time. Automation is appropriate in those cases. But in others, it's almost like outsourcing. I think it's often done with less than a concerted effort to improve process in other ways. Like outsourcing, automation shouldn't be a goal, but just a tool.

When considering outsourcing or automation, it is best to pay heed not only to the Scarecrow, but also his partners, the Tin Man and the Cowardly Lion.

A High-Performance Team Emerges

All this change that we accomplished was not just about the knowledge of the Scarecrow. It was also about the heart of the Tin Man and the courage of the Cowardly Lion.

That production operator who was so enthused about the Kanban implementation wasn't alone. As we solved problems and made ourselves and our customers happier, the team became ever more confident, and morale soared. Successful process improvement efforts became the expectation and the norm. From my view, a general calmness, pervasive optimism and greater professionalism seemed to suffuse the team's decision-making and daily activities.

One day early in my tenure, a production operator had come to me. Her supervisor was out, and she wanted approval to scrap a production lot, due to test failures of parts in that lot. I began to ask questions. What was the criterion for declaring a lot to be scrap? It turned out that each of the supervisors had been using a different rule of thumb. None of them had an economic model to follow.

That very day, I created a one-page decision analysis form for the supervisors and asked them to use it from then on. The model was a simple worksheet that compared the price of a finished product with the incremental cost of completing the lot, accounting for the expected yield loss. If the lot would cost more to complete than the money we'd get for it, then the lot ought to be scrapped. On the other hand, if we'd get more money than the completion would cost, then we ought to finish it. The form wasn't a difficult thing to use, it would reduce variability in decisions, and having a body of such completed forms would give us another learning tool.

A few weeks later, when another production operator came to me, asking for a scrap approval, I asked for the worksheet, but she hadn't heard of it. It seemed that the supervisors had ignored my direction on this issue. So I took a few minutes to fill out the worksheet for this particular case in front of the operator. It so happened that the lot in question was worth completing, so I declined to sign the scrap sheet.

The operator seemed enthralled by the worksheet. "Can I have one of these?" she asked.

I smiled. "Absolutely. And please share it with your teammates. I'd like to see these used in the future."

"Oh, we will!" she replied.

"I'll make the electronic version available to everyone, so anyone can print it and use it. And if there's anything else about the business that you'd like to know, please feel free to ask me anytime."

Thus, I made my end run around the supervisors, and I let them know it at our next staff meeting, too, in no uncertain terms. This incident supported my instinctive desire to educate the operators to the point where we would require fewer supervisors.

Step-by-step, process variability gave way to uniformity and process control. Eventually, our main frustration came down to the fact that customers would often change order quantities after we'd released new lots into production. This was yet another source of variability that would wreak some havoc on our production schedule. Our lead time was down to about a month at that point, and we felt very proud of that accomplishment, but it seemed that we were still at the mercy of the customers' schedule uncertainty.

I asked our production control specialist to analyze these change orders, and she reported that very few happened within two weeks of the eventual delivery dates. In other words, customers were pretty good at forecasting their requirements up to two weeks out, but not longer.

At a department meeting, I posed this what-if: What if we could start and finish each production lot in less than two weeks? Then we'd seldom see a change order from a customer! It seemed simple in concept but a serious challenge in reality. Nonetheless, the team had created so much success that they were not daunted.

In fact, they assumed that challenge with great enthusiasm. It was a clear goal, with clear benefits. The effort proceeded with the discipline of a military campaign. Over a few months, our lead time shrank to 10 working days. They had hit the goal. They did it without overtime work, without any hiring, and without any other trick work-arounds. It was accomplished by continued quality improvement and process improvement. I was extremely proud of the team.

But they didn't stop there. They realized that they could keep improving lead time through the factory. Over several months, that important metric dropped to just 6 days, and the team foresaw ways to shrink it even further.

By this time, on-time delivery had long ago reached 100%, and customer returns for quality issues were rare. With a streamlined new product introduction process, new product samples could be delivered in a few days. In one emergency case, we took a revised design from a customer and delivered samples in one shift. Meanwhile, our prices to our internal customers had dropped by a large fraction during all these improvements, reflecting our decreasing costs.

Our customers were astounded and extraordinarily pleased by the department's turn-around. We had made their jobs that much easier. As a result, our business, which had been shrinking by about 5% per year, was now growing by about 15% per year.

In mid-1994, about two years after Roger and I had assumed the management of the thin film department, Roger decided to take a position at another HP division, and I became production manager for the entire department.

Right around that time, we took the next step: self-directed teams.

When They're Ready for Self-Direction, They'll Demand It

When I took over the test and separation group, we were running three shifts, five days a week, with three supervisors. The shifts didn't get along very well. The night shift claimed to be the most productive, but I had my doubts. I put some metrics in place to find out, and these confirmed that the night shift was the least productive. Shortly after, I directed that this shift be eliminated, but I gave each worker on that shift a choice of joining either the day or evening shift, except for the supervisor, who was transferred to another department. The result was that production on the other two shifts increased more than enough to make up for the loss of the night shift.

As the team developed, and in the wake of the demand-pull training, various informal leaders appeared in the organization. They had always been there, the standouts, but now they took on more formal roles, with some encouragement from the supervisors and me. We divided the production operation informally into work cells, based on closely related processes, and these leaders became the coaches and organizers of the work cell teams. This approach left less of a need for formal supervision, and I eventually eliminated one of the remaining separation and test supervisor positions, moving the remaining incumbent into a split-shift schedule. We did similarly in the fab.

So we were left with just two production supervisors in the department. Their roles changed dramatically as a result of the shifts in responsibility and the extensive education of their staffs. The supervisors naturally transitioned into roles of coaching and facilitating the continuing enhancement of their team members' skills and opportunities. Very little of their own time went into firefighting, but their experience and overview was helpful to team problem-solving activities.

The supervisors and their teams developed a system for training in which operators could request training and certification to perform a specific operation that they weren't already familiar with. Over time, performance rankings would reflect the number of operations that a person was certified on, because that metric drove increased flexibility in our operations.

I have not mentioned the thin film department engineering team already, and that's an oversight. When I took over the separation and test group, it had about five engineers reporting to me. They were very frustrated and felt abused at that point. I asked them each to give me a simple analysis of their individual time use, and the results immediately showed the source of their dissatisfaction: They reported that they spent about 97% of their time fighting fires in production, and only the remainder working on process improvement or new product development.

So, as the production operators had become more educated on both the business and their processes, Roger and I had directed a transition as I had in the magnetics group. The operators became the owners of their processes, with the engineers becoming their technical consultants and coaches. It worked. Within a year, the same questionnaire produced the opposite response: The engineers were spending only about 3% of their time fighting fires. Their effort had shifted to pursuing innovations in the products and processes, as well as technical education and coaching of the operators. These were roles that the engineers enjoyed immensely.

After I took responsibility for the fab as well, I had a total of nine engineers reporting directly to me, along with the two production supervisors, a prototyping supervisor and an equipment maintenance supervisor. To put this in perspective, we had begun with a total of 14 managers, including me, in the operations that I led. By this time, our team had shrunk from over 100 people to fewer than 60, producing nearly twice as many circuits per month than before we had started our turn-around. So we had created a productivity increase of nearly a factor of four. Those supervisors and their teams knew how to run the business effectively. I was starting to have more of that time for golf, and once again, I loved it. I viewed my job as working myself out of a job, based on creating a high-performance team.

Overall, things in my boss's department had improved to the point that, when he decided to move on, a replacement wasn't needed. I was promoted to production manager, a senior management position, reporting to one of the division's two manufacturing managers.

I began participating in an HP-wide Work Innovation Network, an informal group of managers who were experimenting with new ways of organizing work and rewards systems. It was timely for me, as I began to think about taking our department further by transitioning to self-directed teams. I learned much from the network and began to think about a new rewards system for production workers, one in which their base pay would be based on their demonstrated level of knowledge, and the team would split a bonus based on the overall team's performance on the important business metrics. I hoped to do something analogous for the engineers, although this kind of change would likely be more difficult to implement, due to the company's performance management policies and procedures for "professional" employees.

Several weeks after beginning these investigations, I happened to mention my thoughts to a few people. To this day, I'm not sure whether doing that was a mistake or a stroke of genius. The next thing I knew, the production operator teams were rife with speculation that we were shifting to self-direction. People came to me, volunteering to help. They wrested the idea away from me. And I realized that, whether I was ready or not, they were.

If they're ready for self-direction, they'll demand it. Shifting to self-direction before the team was ready would have been an abandonment of leadership responsibility, from my view. I had seen an example or two of such circumstances, and they hadn't worked out well. So I had carried a reluctance to let go. It was a bit of a shock, then, to realize that the people were ready, that they really did know how to run the business well. Mentally, I repeated my mantra, "Give up control to get control."

Just about that time, my new manager left to become the general manager of another division. I would now report to the remaining manufacturing manager. I am certain that the improvements made in my own department not only enabled us to reduce the number of management positions within that department but also made possible the higher-level streamlining.

My new manager, Jerry, made a show of being very skeptical of my department's reported business results. It seemed that he didn't understand how we'd achieved those results, and so he questioned the data.

Very soon, Jerry asked me for a tour of the thin film operation, and I gladly set him up with a supervisor. I trusted my team implicitly, so I saw no reason to spend my time on the tour. About two hours later, I came upon him talking with a couple of the fab operators. He had just completed the tour. I smiled at the thought that the supervisor had also delegated the tour at some point.

I waited nearby for them to finish their conversation, and then I approached him.

"How'd the tour go?" I asked.

"I'm amazed at how much your people know about the business!" Jerry exclaimed, with both puzzlement and admiration in his tone.

"That's why we're successful!" I replied.

My team had developed to the point that they didn't need me anymore. I'd worked myself out of the job, and I had even more time for golf. It was time to seek new opportunities to practice and extend what I'd learned about leadership in the manufacturing environment.

I felt ready for a position of greater responsibility. However, the recent management reorganization had left me with nowhere to go inside the division.

After some exploration, I decided to move into HP's Strategic Business Development group, which would give me the opportunity to consult on process improvement to executives of other companies. I was eager to apply my skills and knowledge in that way. I joined my new team in early 1995 and gave up my office at HP's Santa Rosa site to work from home and from the sales office in Mountain View. Thus began a new phase in my career and a wonderful new segment of my Yellow Brick Road.

***

About two years later, I happened to be back at the Santa Rosa site for a sales meeting and stopped for lunch in the cafeteria. There I spotted one of the engineers who'd reported to me in the thin film department and asked if I could join him for lunch. We had a nice time getting reacquainted, and eventually I asked how things were going in the department, in which he still worked.

"They're going great," he said. "We're producing about twice as many circuits as we did when you left."

I was pleased to hear of that prodigious business growth, and I was curious. "How many people were added to accomplish that?"

"Oh, maybe two or three."

"Really!" I was genuinely astonished. "How did they increase productivity so much?"

He shrugged and said, "We just kept doing what you taught us."

I basked in a moment of management heaven.

Design for Cycle Time

Gradually, I came to think of everything in terms of lead time, or rather, as it's commonly called now, *cycle time*. There had always been a lot of talk in our factories about "design for manufacturing," "design for test," "design for support," and so on. We finally started calling all of that "design for X," meaning everything that everyone talked about. But that always dissatisfied me, because it didn't represent a unified principle, but rather a large set of objectives and tactics. Fortunately, cycle time came to my rescue.

Before I go on bandying that term about, as if I have no regard for its feelings, let me explain that *cycle time is today's common term for the total time required to produce a product in a factory, including both processing time and waiting (queuing) time.* Now, at the risk of being picayune about it, I will point out that the good people who work in the fields of operations management and production control call this parameter "throughput time" or, sometimes, "factory lead time" or "manufacturing lead time." Formally, in their parlance, "cycle time" is, instead, the interval between successive product completions, as one might witness at the end of an assembly line. But we are conversing in the common tongue here, so with a tip of our hats to those good people, we will dare to employ the common meaning of *cycle time.* Enough about that.

Recalling my original passion for understanding how to create a product that satisfies everyone involved, I realized that the ultimate principle and practice that I was seeking is what I call "design for cycle time." By this, I mean that one must first achieve quality through proper application of the concepts of design for manufacturability and other factors, and the processes of statistical process control, and all the other concepts of world class manufacturing and lean manufacturing. But once those fundamentals are in place, then the result ought to be the achievement of *minimum cycle time in both product development and manufacturing.* In this regard, I am referring to "yielded" cycle time, reflecting the lost time due to less-than-perfect performance.

Note that I am conceptually extending the concept of cycle time into the product development realm, where it can live quite comfortably, indeed. A discipline of lean product development has emerged, and it reflects this kind of thinking. A greatly elaborated analysis of this idea is presented in *The Principles of Product Development Flow: Second Generation Lean Product Development,* by Donald G. Reinertsen,[9] particularly in regard to exploiting creative variability.

To achieve such a result, the effort must include not just the product itself, but the organization that produces it. The organizational structure and processes must support the fastest possible results, consistent with achieving adequate process control and quality of results. In planning the turn-around of our thin film circuit production operation, Roger and I knew instinctively that we needed to pursue these organizational goals along with the technical process goals.

Also, it's important to understand that reducing cycle time is not just a cost-reduction approach. It is fundamentally also a revenue-increasing strategy. Production that is faster, more reliable, more flexible and more responsive to changing customer needs can drive increased demand for the company's products. Roger and I witnessed this effect in our thin film circuit production transformation.

So I summarize all this as *design for cycle time*. If you do everything right with the product and with the organization, then things will happen quickly and with delightful results. That's what I learned from my turn-around experiences. Design for cycle time.

After I grasped this unifying principle, I applied it in every operation I ran and every executive consultancy I performed. It became surprisingly easy to spot the symptoms of dysfunction. I just had to look for where time was being lost in production or back in the development process. Then it was a matter of figuring out why that was occurring, and how to solve it. I began to tell clients that their factories were gold mines, because they would prosper if they figured out how to shrink the queues that seemed to sprout everywhere.

This principle isn't limited to processes that produce gadgets. I led my European consulting team through a similar analysis of our own processes, in an effort to reduce the cycle time for identifying and winning clients. Later on, as an independent consultant, I applied the same principle successfully to help a grant writer improve her business's efficiency and profitability. Process is process, after all.

When a Little Knowledge is Dangerous

Continuing our exploration of manufacturing, let's come back for a moment to knowing which knobs to turn, and the care that must be exercised in balancing changes in technology, products, processes, and people.

In the spring of 1997, I was consulting to Space Systems/Loral, a major manufacturer of commercial communications satellites. The subject, once again, was how to make satellite integration and test faster and less expensive. The investigation took me through the entire factory, as usual, and I found problems not only in integration and test but also in upstream production of subsystems.

Often, in a factory, we find the presence of professional expediters. These folks have the unenviable job of advocating for particular customers and projects, creatively and competitively moving their work ahead of others' in order to accelerate their own product delivery. Expediters have been particularly prevalent in aerospace businesses. More to the point, they are prevalent in factories where processes are out of control and clogged with work-in-process inventory. In such environments, product movement through the factory can be positively glacial, and so managers try to mitigate the problem through expediting. The leadership of Space Systems/Loral found itself in that position but showed no signs of understanding the underlying causes. Hence, my consultancy.

If one is inclined to improve the underlying factory processes in such an environment, so as to reduce or eliminate the need for expediting, it is imperative to recognize first that expediting *is* the process that keeps the factory moving in these cases.

A few weeks into the Space Systems/Loral project, I already knew most of what I would propose as a solution set. It was to be a very broad program, involving many aspects of the work, not just test processes. Implementation of the solutions would have to be a very carefully regulated effort, so as not to further destabilize the factory as improvements were made.

As usual, I made an appointment with the chief financial officer to get his perspective on things. I find that good CFOs usually have an accurate sense of where the problems are. They must count on other executives and their teams for solutions.

After a general discussion of the status of my work, I asked the CFO what he thought of the situation in the factory. He said, "Well, structurally, I would say that we have about 200 people too many for our level of revenue." That was a relatively easy thing to deduce from the financial numbers, and although my access to those figures was restricted, I had no reason to dispute his comment.

Then it was his turn to ask me what I had found. Among other things, I told him of my findings in regard to work-in-process inventory. There was so much built up, in circuit boards and other bits and pieces, that none of it would actually be integrated into satellites for many months or even years. In fact, most of those items awaiting integration would be subject to multiple engineering change orders before integration, requiring them to be modified and rebuilt multiple times, and thereby incurring increasing reliability risk. I explained the futility and excess expense of beginning the assembly of these units so far in advance of the factory's actual capacity to use them, even if the formal schedule called for it.

To reinforce the point, I mentioned the presence of expediters that I'd noticed and casually asked the CFO how many expediters there were in the factory. "One hundred seventy-five," he answered, and then his face went briefly slack, while he stared past me at nothing.

Oh, no, I thought. *Oh, no.* I knew what he was thinking. Eliminate 175 expediters, and you've eliminated most of the 200 people that you need to lose.

Now I had a moral and business dilemma. Do I warn him, or do I hold my place as a consultant and wait to see what happens? In the next few moments, I squirmed internally like a bug on a pin. If he laid those people off, then I would get the chance to see a real-life leadership experiment unfold before my eyes. The company might learn a valuable lesson, but I might be blamed for the inevitable bad ending. I might end up with a target on my back. On the other hand, if I warned him, he might resent it, and I might lose my access and damage my project.

In the end, I decided that it wasn't my place to warn him. I decided to remain silent and let events unfold. I thanked him for his time and ended the meeting.

The next day, sure enough, I got the word that Space Systems/Loral had laid off its expediters. All of them. I resolved to stay away from the factory for a while.

Some days later, I heard that the result of the lay-off was that the factory had virtually stopped. No one had known what to work on.

The expediters had been the process for deciding that, as I had known.

I understand that, within a week, most of the expediters had been recalled and put back to work. Lesson learned. But the poor survivors were going to have to work that much harder.

I was able to re-enter the factory soon after and found that I had not been blamed. My discussion with the CFO was never mentioned in my presence.

THE TIN MAN

"I can fairly hear my heart beating!"
— The Tin Man

He stands in a forest, rusted in place, unable to move. Dorothy and the Scarecrow free him with an oil can. He believes he is incapable of love and compassion because his hollow chest lacks a heart. Nevertheless, he shows unfailing love and compassion for those around him, throughout the quest. Is he not human after all?

Continuing My Journey on the Yellow Brick Road

When we left off the story of this journey, I was nearing completion of my Caltech education as an aerospace engineer and my first step toward becoming a leader in a leading-edge technological organization. However, for people like me, times were tough. The aerospace industry was enduring an extended business slump. I remember laid-off aerospace engineers and managers coming into my parents' bakery looking for even menial work. They expressed their fear that their children would starve. It was a terrible thing to witness, even if I hadn't been poised to follow in their professional footsteps.

93

Just before the holidays in the winter of 1972, the program I worked in at JPL was cancelled by NASA, and many of the technicians and engineers in my group were notified that they would be laid off in June of 1973. I was on the list, and I would lose my job just as I was to receive my Master's Degree.

I began applying for jobs and enduring interviews. In the end, I was fortunate to have 7 offers in the aerospace and energy fields. JPL eventually offered me a job doing mission planning and planetary gravitational-assist trajectory analysis for the first spacecraft mission to the outer planets, a project that eventually was named "Voyager." It was my dream job. But by then, I understood something about how the aerospace business was structured, and its stunning mass migrations of employees in pursuit of new projects. How cruel and wasteful it seemed! Newly married, I decided that I couldn't bank my career on that industry. After all, how many places in the world need someone who can plot a course to Saturn?

I took a job as a jet engine preliminary design engineer with a company in Los Angeles. It paid well, but the place felt like an engineering sweat shop, and that convinced me even more to look outside the industry. I left that job for greener pastures after just 6 months.

In the wake of the OPEC oil embargo of early 1973, the US electric utility industry had come together to pool its resources devoted to R&D on advanced technologies for power generation, transmission, distribution and storage. Late that year, I joined the newly established Electric Power Research Institute (EPRI), as a project manager in advanced technologies for fossil fuel electric power generation and electromechanical energy storage. This work involved not only the technical tasks of project definition, contractor selection and project management, but a considerable amount of leadership in related program definition, technical societies, international collaborations, and advice to Federal legislators. I had no employees reporting directly to me. My R&D projects were all carried out through contractors in industry and universities. It was a bureaucratic job, but at least it had some technical content, allowed me to be creative in designing projects, and taught me some valuable lessons in working with many kinds of managers, executives and politicians.

In the spring of 1974, when I was just 23 years old and still wet behind the ears, I found myself in Butte, Montana, as the utility industry's chosen expert on MHD, an experimental method for generating electric power that offered improved thermodynamic efficiency over conventional plants. I was brought to a hotel meeting room with just a few people in it, so that I could be introduced to Mike Mansfield, the legendary Majority Leader of the United States Senate, who was born in Butte and represented Montana in the Senate. This technology was important to him for a number of reasons, not the least of which was an opportunity he was pursuing to secure Federal investment in research facilities in Montana. I was there to advise that effort from a technical standpoint, amid roiling political forces in the wake of the OPEC oil embargo.

EPRI's governmental liaison in Washington, DC, Mr. Jack Guy, who also happened to be from Butte and had known Mansfield for many years, walked me up to the Senator and introduced me to him as a man "of impeccable integrity." Mansfield, a man of small physical stature and piercing blue eyes, a living legend, seemed to look right through me to my very soul. I remember my knees shaking when he reached out to take my hand. It remains the only time I have ever felt intimidated by anyone, and he wasn't even trying. I think the Cowardly Lion would have turned tail and run, but I found my courage in that moment. I stood there, met his gaze head on, and smiled. I believe that this introduction meant a great deal to my future fortunes in that field of research.

In the fall of 1976, at the request of the US Departments of Energy and State, I represented the US electric utility industry in an official visit to Moscow in support of the US-USSR Cooperative Program in Magnetohydrodynamic Power Generation. This meeting was part of the technical exchange program that had been negotiated between President Nixon and Premier Brezhnev amid an ostensible lessening of Cold War tensions called "Détente." The visit was a grueling week of negotiations and technical symposium sessions sandwiched between visits to the ballet and opera in Moscow, lavish dinners and working lunches. I co-chaired a session of the symposium with a Soviet scientist, and I participated in the negotiations over future collaborative engineering experiments. For a year afterward, I couldn't look at a bottle of vodka without shivering.

In 1977, I spent three months on loan as Deputy Director of Technology of the Montana Energy and MHD R&D Institute, in Butte. Jack had called to tell me that the managing director of the new institute, Dr. Jerry Plunkett, had suffered a cardiac event, and that the Honorable Mike Mansfield, Majority Leader of the United States Senate, had requested the favor of my taking over until his recovery. I knew that the idea probably didn't emerge exactly that way, but how could a 26-year-old say no?

But then, it emerged that the cardiac event was merely an attack of angina. Jerry was back on the job after several days. But he called to tell me that his deputy had been tapped by the governor of Montana for a state position and asked if I would still come to fill in that position. It would still make the Majority Leader happy, apparently.

I agreed but arranged for a fixed-term assignment, so that there would be no question of this being a try-out for a permanent move. Michelle and I relocated to Butte with our one-year-old son and our cat. We lived in a farmhouse eight miles out of town, on the Continental Divide, across the Helena Highway from a dairy farm. It wasn't an easy time, and Michelle had the worst of it, although the people, the town and the state were delightful.

This brief position afforded me a unique opportunity to observe and influence the interactions of Federal, state and industry programs around the installation of a major experimental test facility in Butte. I remember making frequent trips from Butte to Washington, on the "Mansfield Special," an airline flight that spent most of the day hedgehopping across Montana and the Dakotas, to finish in Minneapolis in time to catch a nonstop flight to Washington. On one visit, I brought Senator Mansfield a gift of a case of canned Truzzolino tamales, his favorite, made in Butte, for which he was grateful.

Meanwhile, I had been working on the idea of getting myself loaned out to a utility company in order to get the field experience in power plants that I was missing. If I were going to stay in this industry, I needed that credibility.

After my return to Palo Alto in the summer of 1977, I accepted a two-year assignment to Portland General Electric Company, in Oregon. I would spend nine months as a plant engineer at a "combined cycle" power plant incorporating a new steam turbine unit powered by the exhaust gasses from gas turbine units. Then there would be another nine months as a startup engineer for the coal yard of a new coal-fired steam turbine power plant. I would finish up with six months as a long-term power generation capacity planner in the company's Portland headquarters.

Including the stint in Butte, Michelle and I moved our household six times in 2½ years. Again, she had the worst of it. The cat was none too happy, either. We got so blasé about the moves that neither of us thought of calling the moving company to arrange the last move, until just two weeks before the event.

Those were challenging assignments in Oregon, and I learned a great deal. I came back to EPRI in 1979, with no further questions from my industry colleagues about the adequacy of my understanding of power plant operations and power generation planning.

I also came back with a strong desire to move into technology development that was more near-term, closer to commercial introduction. I had seen the gulf that existed between the heady world of new technology development and the everyday grittiness of getting equipment installed and making it run reliably in the field.

I knew that gas turbine technology had an important place in EPRI's plans, and I aimed to get involved in solving practical problems in that area upon my return from the loan assignment. EPRI's management team had similar ideas, and I became the project manager in charge of gas turbine reliability improvement. It was a great experience over the following two years, with immediate practical results in the field. I found that immensely satisfying.

I hadn't left the MHD field without a last attempt by some powerful people to keep me there. Late in 1979, I received a call from the Director of the Office of MHD within the US Department of Energy. He offered me the position of Director of the Systems Engineering Division, reporting to him. I was flattered, and I thought that fundamental changes were needed in that division. Being all of 29 years old and no spring chicken anymore, I asked what freedom I would have to run the division in the manner that I thought it needed to be run. I already knew the answer. "All the freedom that the political situation allows," he said. I responded that this was exactly the reason that I was declining the offer. He laughed and told me that he thought I was making a wise decision, but that he had felt obligated to offer me the position. He then proceeded to unload his frustration about the politics roiling around government investments in energy R&D, and especially MHD.

That very Director of the Office of MHD lost his position after the 1980 Presidential election, in an extensive purge of Executive Branch positions. I was told later that my name had come up as a possible replacement, which would have required Senate approval, but that I was simply too young. In retrospect, even though I was feeling like I was already on the right track for my career, I don't know whether my ego would have let me turn that one down. Good thing they didn't offer it.

By then I had realized that I would not want a career inside the Washington Beltway, anyway. I knew that my place was in industry. But those several years of work gave me some insight into the workings of Washington agencies and politics, insight that was particularly harsh in the years following not only the oil embargo, but the Watergate scandal.

My experiences in the electric utility industry had shown me the vast chasms that can exist between the presumptions of product developers and the everyday realities of the people who buy their products. Over the years, I developed a curiosity and a passion for the processes that would take a concept and turn it into a product that satisfied investors, customers, employees, and everyone else. I continued to dream of participating in the leadership of such an organization.

But technology changes rather slowly in the utility industry, mainly because of the enormous investments involved in deploying new technology across so vast an infrastructure. So I decided that I needed to go to an industry that could show me faster product life cycles, if I were going to satisfy my professional passion. In 1981, I started that search. We'll pick up that part of the story later.

Meanwhile, let's see what the Tin Man has to say about the place of love and compassion in leadership.

A Leader is a Teacher

Uncovering the role of love and compassion in the leadership of an organization is not always easy and can be downright unpleasant, especially when that role is suppressed. Once revealed, however, that role can offer fertile ground for operational improvement.

I was still in the middle of my consulting engagement at Space Systems/Loral in 1997, and I had run again into some of the symptoms of interpersonal abuse that I found rampant in aerospace companies. I had interviewed Mary, the supervisor of an assembly team that produced the lower-level circuits and other bits that usually sat in work-in-process inventory for an agonizingly long time. I tried to focus her interview on the mechanics of the technical and organizational processes that led to such unsatisfactory results. However, along the way, Mary had used most of a box of facial tissues, as she had cried freely. (I had learned long previously to bring a box or two of tissues with me on interview days.)

This woman had given up a teaching career in the public schools in order to pursue what she thought would be a better career in the space industry. After several years, Mary was profoundly unhappy. She reported feeling that her job was to try to defend her team from the whims of the management, that they were never rewarded but only reprimanded and saddled with more work, and that there was no hope of improvement. Hers had not been an isolated view among the people that my team had interviewed.

One day some weeks later, Mary happened upon me in a hallway, said that she was on her way to her staff meeting, and asked if I would mind attending it for a while. She wanted me to talk about my project and communicate some hope to her team. This was, of course, way outside my duties and privileges as a consultant. But as a friend and as an experienced first-level, mid-level and senior manager who had coached many teams, I said I'd give her a few minutes. I knew that I could keep the conversation from straying into inappropriate discussion.

As we walked toward her meeting room, Mary said, "You know, I'm about ready to quit. I think I'd like to go back to teaching. For me, that was so much more rewarding than being a manager."

We walked a few more steps in silence before I replied. "That's interesting, because what I've found is that managing *is* teaching."

She stopped walking so quickly that I had gone on a couple more steps and had to return to where she stood, staring at me. I waited.

After a few moments, she nodded. "Point taken."

We proceeded to her meeting. What I observed there is that her relationship with her employees was, in fact, that of a teacher with students. She just hadn't realized that she'd brought that style with her to her supervisory job.

More deeply, what I observed was that Mary genuinely cared about these people, and she showed that in the way she communicated with them. It was not paternalistic, but it was, in a way, loving. It may sound corny, but it seems to me that leadership can be practiced in mistrust and anger, or it can be practiced in openness and kindness. The former is an act of fear, while the latter is an act of courage. We have all seen both but may not have recognized them at the time.

What does this mean in the context of a manager's vocational duty to achieve operational and financial objectives? Leaders achieve their goals through the actions of others. It has been adequately demonstrated in research that leading from fear begets more leading from fear, with the result that the team's creativity and productivity are stifled. Leading from courage, as I'm defining it here, can unleash those very attributes in the team.

How does one lead from courage? It starts with loving the role of leader and being comfortable in it. It continues with respecting the people working for you; after all, if you don't respect them, why are they still working for you? In terms of action, leading from courage means setting expectations for employees clearly and firmly, and monitoring the progress without hovering. It means giving employees sensible leeway in how they achieve their objectives, and the ability to do that is enabled by first teaching them as much as possible about the business, and not just their little piece of it. It means tolerating (and even smiling at) mistakes when they are made within the bounds of acceptable practice. It means that the leader can open herself to criticism and ideas from team members. Making oneself open to criticism does not imply a lack of courage; rather, it requires courage and some humble self-confidence!

Then again, sometimes leading from courage means imposing some discipline or moving someone out of a job when their performance is inadequate and is not likely to reach an adequate level in a reasonable time.

Over the many years I was with HP, the division human resources departments would periodically run surveys of employees. Every time, the top criticism of the company was that it tolerated poor performance. Some people referred to this phenomenon as "terminal niceness." This tolerance had a devastating effect on the performance of individual teams and their trust in the company. It belied all the usual buzzwords about valuing performance and striving to be our best.

In a great company like HP, how did this tolerance of poor

performance arise? From my view, which I stated in many meetings (not necessarily to my immediate career advantage), it arose from coaching of supervisors that typically left them feeling that they were responsible for helping employees to solve their performance problems, and from a subtle message that having to fire an employee somehow constituted a failure on the part of the supervisor in that process. Not everyone agreed with me as to cause, of course.

Nevertheless, the result was that chronic poor performers would bounce from group to group within the company, often within a single division. I resolved that any such employee in my group would not be transferred out. Either their performance problem would be resolved on the job, or they would be invited to leave the company. Although not one-hundred-percent successful in this, over time my department became known for permanently resolving employee performance issues. And eventually, good performers from other groups would often approach the supervisors or me to ask if they could transfer into our department.

Achieving this change wasn't as difficult as it might seem. I began by changing the message to my supervisors: Their job was to solve business problems and optimize the business performance of their teams. They were free to invest time in helping poor performers to improve, while understanding that they were risking at least a part of their own professional futures in the process. I would coach a supervisor to carefully weigh the magnitude of a problem, the likelihood of success, the amount of time that they would have to invest in coaching or disciplining the poor performer, and especially the impact on the overall team's morale and performance in the meantime. While doing this, I was constantly teaching the supervisors more and more about the business itself, so that they would have a fuller context in which to make their decisions.

By the way, I had learned this lesson about solving performance problems the hard way, shortly after taking charge of the magnetics group that I described earlier. One of the production operators, a young man with a history of poor behavior, had flung a metal chair across the production lab in anger, frightening several coworkers. Considering this behavior unacceptable and a firing offense, his supervisor and I took him to Human Resources, where one of their representatives took us to a windowless room they informally called "The Bunker."

I proceeded to chastise this man for his awful behavior, which had threatened not only other employees but very expensive, delicate production equipment. With the supervisor's adamant concurrence, I told the HR representative to prepare termination papers, but she took me out of the room and proceeded to talk me out of firing this man. My courage failed me, and I made the mistake of letting her persuade me to put him on probation.

A terrible mistake, that. We sent him home for the rest of the day, but when it was reported back to the team that this man would return in the morning, they were devastated. And they were right to be. The decision impacted their trust and confidence in me and left them afraid of further incidents. I had impugned my own authority as a leader and a teacher. And the supervisor suffered similarly.

Afterward, the man behaved reasonably well but continued to demonstrate mediocre performance for the next several months, while being shunned by his teammates. About six months later, he finally quit the company on his own. His teammates had achieved what I had failed to do. I learned my lesson, I apologized to the team, and I vowed never again to let the "Terminal Niceness Department" talk me into that kind of decision.

Leading from courage includes being tough. It's all in how it's done. Always keep in mind the greater good of the team, its business performance, and how you want the team to develop.

On the other hand, leading from fear can take many forms but is often focused on short-term, localized control and results. We'll look at an example next.

Money is the Most Powerful Drug

Let's come back to my consultancy at TRW Space Systems, which we discussed earlier. In kicking off our consulting process, TRW's corporate vice president and general manager of the division spoke to a gathering of managers and engineering personnel. Although I was consulting on a military project, one of the things the VP/GM said is that he hoped that this project would teach the company how to be more cost-competitive in the satellite market, because he wanted to win commercial communications satellite business. Specifically, he said that TRW Space needed to decrease its dependency on defense money.

I spent months in their factory doing my research, directing the investigations of my team members, interacting with the client's personnel, and developing my recommendations and proposed plans with help from my team. The Air Force ended up selecting TRW and its team and cited the HP team's work as instrumental to their decision. I was quite proud of that outcome and the additional potential business that it opened up among TRW's team and across other Air Force programs. Although the Air Force eventually cancelled this particular project before engaging in the next phase, the insights that our client had gained did help them to improve their business, as the VP/GM had hoped.

Over the course of that work, I had personally interviewed perhaps a dozen employees, ranging from the VP/GM and CFO to assemblers and test technicians, and my team members had interviewed many more. I thought I had a good sense of what the client's technical issues were, but just as importantly, I had gained insight into their organizational issues and how those affected and were affected by the performance of the integration and test processes.

On July 23, 1999, after my initial consultancy was complete, I was working on follow-up planning at TRW's headquarters campus in Southern California, which included their satellite integration and test facility. That morning, I was invited to join their employees to view the launch of their latest product from Cape Kennedy, via closed-circuit TV screens in the cafeteria. This satellite was NASA's Chandra X-ray Observatory, which had taken a decade and $1.65 billion dollars to build. Hundreds of TRW people had worked on it, and I think that most of them were in the room, anxiously hoping for a successful launch.

I was standing next to my everyday contact, Chuck, he of the animated factory flow film that I described earlier.

Along with everyone else, we waited through the countdown. Finally, the rocket engines roared to life, and the huge launch vehicle lifted away from the pad. It seemed that no one around us breathed for the first minute, as we watched the rocket arc into the sky. Anxiety and hope were evident on every face, and there were some tears.

An eternity later, the message came across the TV that the satellite had successfully reached orbit. A great cheer and many sighs of relief erupted from the group around me, and I joined in the applause. There were many more tears now.

Chuck looked around the room at his colleagues and commented at the show of pride that the tears evidenced.

I looked at him and said, "How do you know it's from pride? There can be many reasons for tears."

He said, "Well, certainly they're happy that the launch was successful."

"Yes, but it may be that many of these people are crying from relief. For at least some of them, the launch means that the beatings will stop for a while."

He just looked at me, dumbfounded. I said, "Congratulations on a successful launch. We'll have to wait to hear whether the satellite deploys okay. Meanwhile, let's go talk."

We took cups of coffee and went back to his office, which was enclosed and had a door, which I closed behind me. He sat at his cluttered desk, and I took the visitor's chair.

"Look," I said, "in one of my interviews, with an integration shift supervisor, she broke down in tears, telling me that the pressure to finish this project had been horrific. I understood that she's had only two days off in the past year, and those were to give birth to her baby. Now, she knows what project she's moving on to, and she knows that it's already behind schedule, and that what she has to look forward to is more of the same. But for the moment, for her, the beatings have stopped."

Chuck looked at me thoughtfully. "But who's doing the beating?"

"This isn't part of my job, but I know that my work can only affect things a little here, without broader changes to enhance how the company works. I'm basing this not only on my management experience, but also on my past volunteer experience in human services, dealing with things like domestic violence."

I took a long sip of coffee. "Your vice president said it during our kickoff. It wasn't an accident that he said that your company needed to decrease its dependency on defense spending."

Chuck's expression was quizzical. "I don't see what that has to do with it."

"*Dependency* was the key word. Your company is *dependent* on defense money, in the worst sense. In a family where a parent has a drug or alcohol dependency, the rest of the family often is abused. And the worst part is that the children often learn to cope by abusing each other. If the children are beaten by the adults, they often learn to use violence on each other. In the lull after beatings, there's relief. And often, as stress escalates, the abused members of the family will actually provoke the next attack, so that the relief will come that much quicker."

He still had that quizzical look. "Okay, but who's doing the abusing here?"

"Defense money is your company's drug. The money is under the control of the program managers. You could say that they're the pushers. They allocate the money to the organization, engineering, integration, facilities, everything else. They don't report to the factory management. They're separate from it. So they use the allocation process to get what they want to meet their objectives. It's a rather brutal process. It's often abusive. And that abuse flows down the organization, all the way to the bottom. At the bottom, people end up abusing each other, but I believe that the underlying factors are driven by the program managers." I gave him more examples gleaned from my interviews and observations on the factory floor. "It's not really the program managers' fault. It's in the nature of their jobs."

Chuck sat back in his chair. "I never looked at it that way. How did it get this way?"

"Your company's not alone here. I've seen it everywhere I've worked in aerospace organizations. I think it's built into the program matrix structure. The program's overriding objective to satisfy the customer almost inevitably leads to abuse of the delivery organization. And I would say, the program managers feel like they get their share of abuse back as well, but I don't know if that's true or just part of how they live with what they have to do. And by the way, I saw the same thing when I interviewed here in 1973, which is why I turned down TRW's job offer in spacecraft thermal design. So the organization has been this way for at least the past 26 years."

"Okay, I get what you're saying," he said. "Would you be willing to meet with our division's Director of Human Resources to tell her what you told me?"

Having started this project with quite a bit of prior experience with aerospace/defense organizations, I knew that this environment would impose strict limits on my ability to propose balanced changes in technology, products, processes and people. As a consequence, none of the knobs that needed turning would prove easy to turn, and clarifying the cause was my underlying reason for having this conversation.

"Chuck, you're my client, but I've told you this in order to help you as a friend. We're way outside the parameters of my contract here. If we do that meeting, it will have to be a meeting that never happened."

The fear in this organization was insidious and largely unrecognized precisely because it was woven into the very fabric of the organization over decades. In the end, I cannot claim that my observations on the corporate culture resulted in any positive change in that regard.

This problem is a very important one to mitigate early in the life of an organization, because once it takes hold, it becomes rather intractable. Participants in a startup must particularly watch out for the seeds of this problem: Look at the culture of your major investors. Do they truly understand your market, your business concept, and your plans? Do they truly understand the risks? Are they patient enough to let your team follow a well-disciplined risk-reduction process in product development?

Speaking of Program Managers

The foregoing discussion reminds me of one particular negotiation in which I invoked the power of an aerospace program manager. And, I admit, the dark side of that power. But you may laugh at the end, anyway.

Back in early 1998, I was asked to visit Raytheon's division responsible for manufacturing optical sensors. This company became HP's entry point into the TRW military satellite project I described above. Raytheon was to design and build the sensors that would detect and track a target missile's upper stage after engine burnout. Those sensors were the heart of the system.

Our sales manager for this account told me that Raytheon wanted to ask HP to join the bid team in hopes of winning the business. I agreed to a meeting, even though I knew that my company's business model would not allow us to engage in a risky resource investment like that. My objective going into the meeting was to sell our consulting services to the client for this project. And beyond that, I hoped to leverage this engagement into broader engagements with the prime bidder, TRW, and perhaps others among their team members. I believed that there was potential for tens of millions of dollars in consulting business and test solution sales.

Our sales manager and Raytheon's "capture team leader," who essentially filled the role of a program manager during their effort to win the Air Force contract, set up a meeting at their headquarters in Southern California. I went to that meeting with great anticipation.

The program manager was a tall, lean man named Ira, an experienced scientist with an affable, calm manner and a ready sense of humor. He reminded me of those JPL managers who had come to our home when I was a little boy. I liked him immediately.

Ira presented an introduction to the program and gave me a brief tour of those areas of the factory that weren't classified. In return, I made a presentation on our consulting program and methods, along with my initial impressions of Raytheon's challenges and how I thought HP could help. I told Ira that this help could not come in the form of a bidding partnership, but rather as a paid consultancy. (By the way, with my bigger objective in mind, I commented that it would be most helpful to include a couple of TRW's project personnel in the usual interviews, "for perspective," and he agreed that he could try to arrange this. It was that tactic that led to our invitation into TRW's part of the project and, eventually, to the discussion with Chuck about dependency and program management.)

Having recently done another project of similar scope, although not in the satellite field, I had a good idea of the effort that would be required to help Raytheon, and I estimated a price of nearly a quarter-million dollars. Ira did not balk but said that this deal was possible.

We agreed to proceed with contractual language on this basis.

Working with HP's sales team and some test experts from an HP division, I developed the consulting statement of work and business proposal. We submitted that package to Ira several days after the meeting, and it was well received. After a little discussion and refinement, we had a verbal agreement. Ira said he would run it through their contracts department.

Several days later, I got a phone call from a man in the contracts department named Ed, saying that he was reviewing the proposed contract and needed to have justification for the price. I told him that HP did this kind of consulting as a commercial practice, that I had recently done a similar project for a very similar price, and that this was all the justification he'd get.

Ed replied that HP would have to provide internal costs and other financial data, like any defense contractor. I replied that HP would never agree to that, as it was not in the business of being a government contractor, but rather a commercial provider. Even though we frequently sold test equipment and other items and services to government agencies, these transactions were always based on a published commercial price list. In this case, although there was no published price list, we were, nevertheless, quoting this as a commercial service, not subject to audit. Ed said he'd call me back.

I immediately called Ira and told him of the conversation. "Boys will be boys," he replied. "Ed's job is to get a discount, and he's going to try." He asked me to keep him informed.

I had to weigh the enormous potential for business across this Air Force program and the other business it might lead to, against my belief that my company shouldn't have to provide that private financial information to this client. Not to mention that I'd be laughed out of the room if I even suggested such a thing back at the office. I really wanted this project, but you have to know when to walk away.

A few days later, I received another call from Ed. This time, the head of his department was on the line as well. After introducing her, Ed said that Raytheon's policy required HP to provide the price justification he was seeking. And then he used his ultimate threat: "I'd hate to be in a position of having to tell you that we couldn't approve the contract because we didn't receive that data."

I felt a brief surge of adrenalin, recognizing that the deal was on the line at this very moment, along with all that possible follow-on business. But I also knew that I had power on my side.

Taking a deep breath, I chose my words carefully and spoke in a deadly calm tone. "Well, Ed, I'd hate to be in a position of having to say, take it or leave it."

A moment transpired in silence, and I imagined Ed exchanging looks with his boss. Sounding a little exasperated, he finally replied, "We'll call you back."

I immediately called Ira and left a message on his line, telling him what had transpired and leaving it with, "Look, you came to me and asked me to do this work. I've given you a fair proposal, but I cannot agree to open our financial books to your company."

Less than twenty minutes later, my phone rang. It was Ed again, sounding beleaguered. "If you can have your contracts department send me a letter verifying what you've told me about your price, we'll be pleased to approve your contract."

"That's splendid," I replied. "I'll take care of that right away. And thank you very much."

"You're welcome. Only, please," he begged, "don't call the program manager anymore."

Listen When the Heart Has an Insight

Now, we can have a look at a manufacturing operation where there was no such dependency as TRW suffered, and where love and compassion were in evidence, even in the hard-nosed decision-making necessary to turn around a struggling operation.

In 1995, I was asked to have a look at the factory of NEC America near Portland, Oregon. The plant produced equipment that was used in fiber-optic communication systems. They were having difficulty with production quality. I met with the General Manager of Operations, Phil, a friendly, greying man who had a close handle on what was happening but was at his wits' end as to how to fix the problems.

This was my first experience working with a Japanese company. The plant's staff comprised an interesting cultural mix, and that fact was to offer me some fascinating challenges during this consulting engagement. The general manager was from Japan, but the next layer of management was composed generally of Americans, including Phil. Below that were middle managers who were Japanese or American, with a variety of ethnic backgrounds among the Americans. The lower levels of the organization were a mélange of nationalities and cultures, but mostly Asian. This aspect of the engagement added a richness that I truly enjoyed and, it would turn out, considerable education.

The production operation built up circuit boards and then integrated those into the instruments that they would sell. The problem, as Phil described it, was that the instruments had a high failure rate in their functional tests, at the very end of the production process. The test technicians ascribed most of the failures to defects on the circuit boards, but the circuit assembly operation took great pride in, and swore to, the quality of their work. Phil was desperate for a way to bring some objective data to bear and agreed to engage in the consultancy.

Per my training and instinct, I was keen to involve upper management in my communications, including the Japanese general manager. Meanwhile NEC, per Japanese practice, appointed a "window" representative, a knowledgeable Japanese engineer named Yoshio, through whom I was to communicate. Yoshio explained that the general manager did not want himself to be visibly involved in the project, so as not to unintentionally influence the plant staff to paint an unrealistically rosy picture of things.

I immediately made the mistake of sending a thank-you message to the general manager and his staff, as well as Yoshio, for the opportunity to engage. I intended it as the only communication involving the general manager. It was a very natural American thing to do, but it prompted a rather angry response from the NEC side. No visibility meant no visibility, even in the distribution of a thank-you note.

That's when I went off to read up on Japanese culture, something I ought to have done first. I deduced that by writing to a larger list of people than just Yoshi, I had unintentionally insulted the "window" himself, by implying that I did not recognize the trust and authority that his management had placed in him, and even worse, I had insulted the judgment of the executives who had chosen him. Oops. Big oops.

So I wrote a carefully written apology to Yoshio only, in which I humbled myself, referring indirectly to my mistake, as delicately as possible, and relaying my thanks to the general manager for keeping himself invisible in the consulting process. I was rewarded with a very cordial message back. I was certain that my apology had been passed up the chain, and that they knew that I'd learned my lesson.

The funny part came when I sent my boss a copy of these communications, so that he might grasp the complexity of the situation. Of course, my message was quite opposite to our training and usual practice of involving customer executives, and it was not the normal American way of business. My boss wrote a response that cast aspersions on my sanity. I replied that he would just have to trust me on this.

In accordance with HP's consulting process, I put together a small team of experts who interviewed about 20 people from throughout the organization, while I collected data from the factory floor in order to construct an analytical model of the flow.

The board assembly process utilized a typical, semi-automated process for placing electronic components on the boards, soldering them into place, and cleaning the finished boards. This operation was followed by a visual inspection and manual repair of identified defects.

I noted that the repair operators did some repair on every board. This consisted of melting individual solder joints with a special heater, and then tweaking the position of the component with tweezers before the solder refroze. Such actions could easily damage components or the electronic traces on the boards, in ways that might not be caught until functional testing or even after failure in the customer's hands. This was a kind of operation that ought to be minimized, but in this plant, it was heavily utilized.

My conclusion was that many of the repairs were likely unnecessary, but that there would be no way to know unless more objective methods than visual inspection were put to use. This was a process crying for automation.

We recommended to the customer that visual inspection be replaced by an X-ray inspection machine, which would measure individual solder joints against statistically developed standards for each joint. Phil objected at first, citing the fact that they had tried an X-ray system in the past, which had just created an engineering bottleneck without solving the problem. But HP produced an advanced X-ray inspection system just for this purpose, which I was convinced could solve the problem if properly employed.

After a great deal of diplomatic back-and-forth, we settled on a lease deal, and the X-ray system was installed. I went off to do other projects, figuring our account manager would keep me informed. However, he was replaced a short time later, without my knowledge, and so the communication link was dropped.

About six months later, it occurred to me to check in on the project, which is when I found out about the change in account manager. I spoke to the new one, who did not know a lot about the situation. So I called Yoshio and first apologized for being out of touch. "I'm glad you called, Paul-san" he said. "It's not so good. I think you should talk with Phil." I took it as a really bad sign that NEC's "window" was shifting the communication to an executive.

I called Phil. "It's not going well at all," he said. "Your X-ray system has become a nightmare for engineering and a bottleneck in production, and I'm about ready to pull it out."

"Before you do anything, please let me come up and have a look at the situation." He agreed, and I was there a few days later.

To perform its job, the X-ray system has to be programmed by an engineer to recognize the shapes of normal solder joints for each component on each board. These are established through statistical analysis of measured joints, and the system includes the mathematical tools to help the engineer do this. From there, the system is able to identify solder joints that don't have normal shapes. Accomplishing this ought to have been a non-problem.

I sat down with the responsible engineer, Yoshio, Phil, and HP's account manager. We discussed the ongoing yield problem, and then I asked them to tell me how the X-ray system had been inserted into the process flow.

The engineer said that the machine was just downstream of the visual inspection and repair station. So they weren't taking statistics on how the automated solder process itself performed, but rather on solder joints that included many that were reworked by hand. Those manually reworked joints would be highly variable.

Using this sequence of process steps, it would be impossible to get meaningful statistics to help the engineer do his job of programming the X-ray system to recognize bad solder joints. I said as much, and the frustrated engineer's face showed relief that someone had understood this.

"You've got to get rid of the visual inspection and repair station if this is going to work," I said, looking at Phil.

"We can't do that. Look, these people take great pride in the quality of their work. They want to make sure that every component is perfectly placed and soldered. It's what they think they're doing."

The NEC people prided themselves on their cultural sensitivity and diversity. They drew on the combined strengths of their people, but in this case, their dedication was causing a problem. The cultural basis of the factory was at the core of this problem, but it was also the core of the company.

The room was quiet for a few moments while I pondered. My brain knew that the problem was the manual tweaking, which was largely unnecessary and possibly damaging to quality. But my heart said that the cultural identity of this plant was also crucial to its success.

"Okay," I said. "The way to solve this is to move the X-ray machine upstream of the visual inspection in the process flow. Let the machine take statistics directly on the soldering process results. Get the machine programmed based on that. Let the inspectors do what they want, but give them the X-ray test results on each board to guide them." I counted on the inspectors eventually to rework only defects identified by the X-ray machine. The solution seemed so simple, but, of course, I was looking at the problem from the outside, which brought a certain clarity.

The NEC people agreed with my suggestion, and the engineer said it would be done immediately. I went home, promising to check back with them in a few weeks.

When the time came, I called Yoshio but didn't get through, so I left a message apologizing and telling him that in the interest of time, I would call Phil directly.

Phil actually sounded excited on the phone. "It worked! The people on the line are doing a lot less rework, and yields at functional test are through the roof. And no more engineering bottleneck. Thank you!"

Yoshio called me later on to thank me and HP. "My pleasure,

Yoshio-san!" I replied.

"I have one more request, Paul-san." He proceeded to tell me that the Japanese general manager's boss, an NEC vice president from Japan, had taken great interest in the project and my approach to achieving quality in production. He had asked Yoshio to see if I would prepare a slide on the subject for his use with NEC executive management in Japan.

If there was one mark of success in a Japanese hierarchy, it was this. The VP would recognize my expertise by including my slide in his presentation and would thereby commit himself to utilizing my ideas. I felt greatly honored. And this step represented a possible path to additional business with the company, something I was always keen to gain.

"Yes, Yoshio-san, I will prepare a slide."

I did so, trying my best to make it amenable to Japanese culture, even to the choice of colors. Yoshio reported a few days after I sent the slide that the VP liked it very much and was very appreciative. It seems he had already used the slide in a presentation. "Paul-san, the vice president now asks whether you would be willing to come to Japan to consult on quality."

Well, this was stunning. It occurred to me that the last American invited to Japan to consult on quality might have been W. Edwards Deming, the great expert on quality who is well-known for his work with Japanese industrial leaders in the 1950s, which catapulted Japan into world-leading product quality. I thought I knew what the Tin Man would have felt like, receiving his testimonial from the Wizard, and the Scarecrow receiving his diploma.

"Yoshio-san, please tell him that I am deeply honored and will discuss this with my managers." I knew that my technical work alone would not have earned me this invitation. Indeed, I believed it was largely a recognition of my willingness to honor the Japanese ways.

As it turned out, I was not allowed by my management to take on this project, because, as I was told, my job was to work in the Americas. HP missed an opportunity, I thought, as did I.

But I was very thankful for my brief education in Japanese business etiquette, for the opportunity to honor the culture of the Oregon plant while positioning that team to achieve higher quality, and for the honor that had been afforded me by the company executives.

These lessons would stand me well when I took on the creation of a European consulting team for Agilent Technologies in 2000. After setting up my office in the Netherlands, I took a class in managing international teams, and it built greatly upon my experience with the Japanese. During the course of my work in Europe, I convened many teams comprising members from all over Europe and the UK. Managing widely varying communication styles was a great challenge, and I often felt that as the American outsider, I provided much of the "glue" that kept the team cohesive. That's not to say that I was completely successful in avoiding mistakes, some of which proved quite embarrassing. But I was always focused on learning how to be more effective in that eclectic environment.

As business continues to become more intensively globalized, it becomes ever more important for team leaders and members to be attuned to cultural variations around the world, especially as they affect business practices. This requires not only relevant knowledge but sincere interest in and appreciation for human cultural diversity. I will not dwell on this point here, because it is already well addressed by many excellent books, consultants and courses.

About a year after the unsuccessful discussions about my going to Japan, I learned that NEC in Japan had adopted HP's X-ray inspection system as a standard process for NEC worldwide, and that this was the first time that the company had adopted a standard based on work done in one of its plants outside Japan. I understand that HP eventually sold quite a number of the systems to NEC.

A long time later, I tried to call Yoshio just to say hello but found that he had been transferred back to Japan. So I called Phil.

"Hi, Paul," he said. "It's good to hear from you."

"How are things going?"

"Really well. You know that the plant's been sold, don't you?"

"What?"

He proceeded to tell me that the plant had achieved record quality levels and on-time delivery, lower production costs, and quicker product introductions. Apparently the X-ray system installation had been the key to generating a lot of other improvements, and I wasn't surprised. But I was surprised, in that light, that the plant had been sold.

"Well," Phil said, "it was a business decision regarding the market. But I want you to know that, because of your work here, NEC got a much higher price for the plant than we would have."

Good enough. My work had brought value to the client. And the plant and its people weren't going away. What those people had learned would stay with them, and HP's reputation with them would remain a positive one. I felt very good about that organization's prospects for at least the immediate future, given their ingrained leadership culture.

Of course, there was always the risk that the plant's new owners would see things differently and make changes that would undermine this leadership culture. I have observed that the leadership style of the top management will eventually dominate the organization's behavior, for better or worse, even when that style is very different from that of the lower levels at the beginning.

Often, but not always, this result flows from the very type of business that the organization is undertaking. This thought leads to our next lesson.

Tell Me What You're Good At

Oftentimes, when I was selling or organizing a consultation with an aerospace/defense company, their executives would tell me that they hoped to gain from me an understanding of how to create a blend of HP's process-focused culture with their own program-focused culture. They understood that HP was successful partly because we relied mainly on divisional organizations that were focused on well-controlled, repeatable processes and product-to-product uniformity. In contrast, their own organizations were focused on accommodating the continually varying requirements of their clients. I think these executives recognized the difficulty of maintaining healthy production organizations in such an environment, as I discussed earlier, and they were searching for a happy medium.

One of the JPL leaders who used to come to my family's home when I was a boy was Dr. Eberhard Rechtin. Eb and his very accomplished and elegant wife, Deedee, became close family friends. He would later head the Defense Advanced Research Projects

Agency and serve as an Assistant Secretary of Defense under the Nixon Administration, reporting to Deputy Secretary of Defense David Packard. When Packard left his government position, he brought Eb to HP as corporate Vice President of Engineering.

A brilliant leader who understood innovation and systems architecting better than anyone else I ever met, Eb was also a very kind man. He advised me at various points in my education and career, whenever I sought his counsel.

At the reception following my father's funeral in 1995, Eb and I spoke at length about my impending move from manufacturing management to the executive consulting group within HP. Long retired from the company, Eb expressed interest and some concern that HP's test and measurement business was adding such services to its core instrument business. He cited HP's roots in creating and manufacturing products in a repeatable, controlled fashion, and he expressed the thought that nowhere in that DNA was any capability for accommodating the kind of process and product variability that such intimate customer relationships would require. "Tell me what you're good at, and I'll tell you what you're bad at," he observed.

Eb was pointing out the flip side of what those aerospace/defense executives were saying. To create a successful customer-intimate solutions business would require profound flexibility in our own organization. As it turned out, working with HP's (and later Agilent's) product divisions to create forward-looking solutions for our customers was the hardest part of my consulting job. And when business cycles periodically turned sour, HP's and Agilent's test and measurement business would predictably retreat from the services business to its roots in making and selling electronic "boxes." That was always a painful and costly ordeal for both my company and its customers.

This discussion, in whatever form it happened, was always fundamentally about what was in the heart of the organization. What the organization did about it in good times was a reflection of the breadth and depth of skill that it had developed, in response to the organization's vision and goals. What unfolded in bad times reflected what the organization had of courage. There was never anything else in an organization's life that drew at once, so fully and so mercilessly, on the attributes of the Scarecrow, the Tin Man, and the Cowardly Lion.

With that, we move on to fully consider the role of courage in leadership.

THE COWARDLY LION

"What makes a king out of a slave? Courage!"
— The Cowardly Lion

He pounces upon Dorothy and her companions in the dark woods, bullying them all until she slaps his nose, at which point he begins to cry. He believes he is contemptible because he lacks courage, and that if he were given a title of respect, he would then be able to show courage. But what kind of courage does he show anyway, before the quest is complete?

Completing My Journey on the Yellow Brick Road

Before considering what the Cowardly Lion has to say, let me tell you about the final portion of my own Yellow Brick Road and, I think, the most important.

By 1980, I had concluded that my future would be neither in the electric utility industry nor in the fickle bureaucratic and political realm surrounded by Washington's Capital Beltway. I had decided to seek an environment where I could observe faster product life cycles, so as to learn what it takes to be fully successful in bringing new concepts to market. Three choices presented themselves: aerospace, the nascent biomedical industry, and electronics. Based on my early experience in aerospace, I wasn't going to go back there. After a search of some months in 1981, I accepted an offer to join a division of Hewlett Packard's Test and Measurement Group, which produced electronic equipment for communication system testing, defense-related testing and surveillance, and similar purposes. I would be starting over as an engineer, but I would be joining one of the world's greatest companies in a fast-moving field.

I started in the division's engineering group that worked with component suppliers. The work was not highly technical, but it gave me a chance to utilize my interpersonal and negotiation skills while learning about this new environment. I became the team's manager after about 18 months and remained in that position for another five years.

With HP's support, I earned an MBA in Management, just to get the book learning to support my real-world experience. That was completed in 1987. Even the Scarecrow needed his diploma, in order to believe that he knew something.

In 1988, I was asked to become a manufacturing section manager in HP's Microwave Technology Division, which manufactured complex, advanced components for use in HP instruments. It seemed an excellent move for me, as it put me in charge of two small component businesses and was a great position in which to practice and grow my leadership skills.

By 1992, I had completed a turn-around of one of these two businesses and had led our exit from the other. I was handed more responsibility, and by 1995, I had completed the implementation of what became known as "lean manufacturing" in another department. I had worked myself out of managerial duties to the point where I could move on again, leaving the group in the hands of a great team.

I was ready for more challenges, but it became clear that there was no opportunity for me to move up within the division.

So I turned to the field sales organization and became a consultant to executives of HP customers, as a member of HP's Strategic Business Development Organization. Eventually I did the same for HP's instrumentation spinoff, Agilent Technologies, ultimately becoming the leader of its worldwide Strategic Business Development team.

I directed much of my consulting work toward companies in aerospace, my first professional love. I eventually consulted to most of the communications satellite manufacturers in the US and, informally, to some European companies. I showed these clients how to speed up and economize the processes of integrating and testing these complex systems, while helping HP and Agilent understand the test equipment architectures that these customers would need for the future. Along the way, I did a short stint in the marketing role of Satellite Market Solution Planner, which had the responsibility for defining the company's market and technology strategies. So my knowledge and experience were put to good use.

In 2000-2002, with all that consulting experience in hand, I transferred to Amsterdam in order to build a European consulting team for Agilent, which I did. Unfortunately, that effort was cut short by both the bursting of the "telecom bubble" and the aftermath of the attacks on the US of September 11, 2001.

I wrapped up some 21 years with HP and Agilent in 2003, when I became a successful independent consultant for a time. One project was for Raytheon Missile Systems, which I performed as a consultant to Agilent, and it proved very successful, with work continuing for years after I departed.

My departure was caused by a diagnosis of asbestos-related cancer. The median post-treatment survival for my cancer was just five years, and that's what I decided to plan for. I was going to do my best to enjoy retirement for the remaining time.

I settled for never having reached my dream of being among the leaders of an organization that brought cutting-edge technologies to fruition. But I had been a trusted consultant to some such leaders, and I resolved to be satisfied with that.

However, it was just a short time later that I agreed to give a couple of years to help start C8 MediSensors, an exciting and worthy cause. I thought I would stay in the background as the Vice President of Business Development, help the venture to get funded, and then back out. But backing out proved impractical, because leading the fundraising ensured that I became the primary liaison with investors. Soon I found myself with the designation of Chief Operating Officer, because institutional investors didn't want to deal with a mere VP. And so I took responsibility for various functional areas of the company, while continuing my personal battle against cancer. In all, the company consumed my professional attention and time for some nine years, spent entirely in leadership positions, including the CEO slot for the last nine months. So in the end, I did achieve my dream, even after having given up on it. Never say never!

In my personal life, I have been an incurable volunteer in non-profit organizations, having run one and served on various boards and a county commission. My wonderful wife, Michelle, and I have also been active as individuals in Washington, DC, fighting to end asbestos poisoning in America, supporting American innovation and competitiveness, and advocating reduction of environmental pollution. We pursue active citizenship, because we believe it's the precious legacy and duty of every American.

Michelle and I raised three wonderful children, who are all married, and two of them have given us a total of six grandchildren. That has been a wonderful education, as well, and a most rewarding life experience.

So that's my personal Yellow Brick Road, except that I have not fully explained the dark episodes that we encountered along the way, just as Dorothy did on her journey to the Emerald City. Of these, the most important is that, in 2004, I was diagnosed with peritoneal mesothelioma, the abdominal form of the asbestos-related cancer. I had documented occupational exposures in the aerospace and utility industries, as well as some exposures at home.

Four surgeries, three kinds of chemotherapy and a new immunotherapy regimen have enabled me to greatly outlast that five-year median survival statistic. But by early 2015, the latest chemotherapy regimen had lost its effectiveness on my disease. The remaining tumors, which were inoperable, spread to my chest and lungs, I became very weak, and by July, it seemed that I had no more than weeks left to live. Michelle and I made final preparations, and I said my goodbyes to friends.

But then I undertook a last-ditch treatment with an experimental medication that aims to boost the body's immune system. Miraculously, within a few months, that treatment had dramatically reduced the tumor masses in my body, and I began feeling healthier and more energetic. As I tell my friends, I feel that I'm in the bonus round of my life.

This battle has been my constant companion as I pursued my consulting project at Raytheon Missile Systems, my first retirement, my long engagement with C8 MediSensors, and now my second retirement, as well as the births of all my grandchildren. From the beginning, as we learned about the terror of asbestos poisoning,

Michelle and I became advocates for the rights of asbestos victims, for improving diagnosis and treatments, and for achieving a ban on trade in asbestos in the US. Those battles have taken us back inside the Washington Beltway many times, where we have helped win some battles but lost others, and where we have made some sincere and powerful friends over the years.

Every moment is precious to me now. I strive to find the potential for good in even the worst of times and to act upon it. I believe it ought to be so for each of us. In the darkest days of my fight against mesothelioma, I found the possibility of sharing my lessons in leadership, technology and life. I feel very fortunate to have survived to fulfill that possibility. The really great thing is that there is plenty more potential for good out there!

So now, let's check in with the Cowardly Lion and see what he has to say about courage in leadership.

Naming the Fear is the First Step

Almost immediately after I presented my analysis of the TRW satellite factory for the Air Force program in California, the Director of Satellite Integration and Test who had engaged my services was replaced. This kind of thing used to happen occasionally, in the wake of my consultancies, as the higher management levels suddenly realized that an outsider had developed a fuller view of the situation and solution paths than the existing functional manager. That is not to say that my work was solely responsible for such decisions; certainly other factors were at work in each case.

Ms. Sonya Sepahban, who took over as Director of Satellite Integration and Test, was already in charge of Systems Engineering, which is the function that defines the mechanical and electronic interfaces between subsystems of the satellite so as to achieve the optimal performance, reliability and cost of the overall system. She was to keep her systems engineering responsibilities while taking on integration and test. That was a good way to work toward breaking down critical communication and process barriers that had developed in the organization. I felt that this new structure was in keeping with the philosophy of my proposed solution path for this client.

I met Sonya the next time I was at the client's site. She struck me immediately as cordial, technically sharp, focused on success and expectant of excellence from those around her. She showed respect for the work I had done, which was refreshing, since many executives resent being "saddled" with a consultant's recommendations. I know that I have felt that way the few times that I was forced to work with a consultant whose intentions or skills I did not respect.

So I was very gratified to have received a friendly and interested reception from Sonya. We spoke about the findings of my analysis and my recommendations for change. She seemed to concur with those results without hesitation and was ready to move into the implementation phase, in which I would closely support her effort to make those changes happen in the factory. It was understood that these changes would have a life of their own, independent of whether the company won the specific military contract it was seeking. The changes were needed anyway, if the company was to lessen its dependency on military spending.

Within a short time, HP's implementation team was ready to move ahead. It included experts on satellite test and test equipment, data systems management, a custom solutions architect, a project manager, and myself. Our sales account team was aligned with the effort, ready to help create purchase orders and work with our technical divisions to provide solutions on schedule and on budget.

From our view, everything was ready to go. However, I began to hear some rumblings from my team that things weren't all roses on the TRW side. There was apparently some resistance to moving forward. Most often this happens when the planned changes cause some or all of the client's personnel to feel threatened in their jobs or in their existing positions of power in the organization. It's to be expected. I always thought of it in an organic analogy: My team and I represented a virus invading the organization, although with favorable intentions, but antibodies would naturally develop as a result of the organization's resistance to change.

There are always antibodies, even if things look good. A good consultant, sales agent, or project manager keeps his or her eye on the corners, looking for the signs, because a well-placed, capable antibody can do a great deal of damage and even destroy a project. Indeed, I believe that there is no organizational strategy that cannot be damaged or destroyed by an opponent, even someone in the lowest position on the organization chart.

I attended a kick-off meeting of Sonya's staff with my team to discuss and further plan the implementation phase. The first part was a review of the various components of the plan. Most of the presentation was made by HP's project manager. Sonya asked a number of questions and made various comments, but her team remained largely silent, and their body language was not encouraging.

We broke for coffee, and the project manager took me aside to note that he sensed fear in Sonya's team. I asked him what he thought was driving that. He told me that Sonya, being new to many of these people, did not have well-developed communications with them, and that they were concerned that they were being asked to take on new tasks without giving up any of their previous ones. There apparently had been no general discussion of this issue in our absence.

I knew that our project and HP's future ability to prosper from this high-level relationship would suffer if we didn't get past this obstacle quickly. So I quietly took Sonya aside and explained the concern. She knew that it was natural for her team to have some reluctance around the changes and asked what I thought should be done. Already understanding that Sonya was a person who did not let her fears unduly influence her decisions, and who was often well ahead of her team in understanding the issues, I realized that she and her team needed an opening to create the needed conversation, to break down the unspoken barriers. I sensed that I was in the best position to create that opening. "Sonya, in this next session, I'm going to create an opportunity for you to open the necessary conversation. I don't exactly know how or when, but you'll know when it happens."

We reconvened. A few minutes later, Sonya was discussing with one of her engineering team leaders a particular element of the project and seeking a schedule commitment. She was getting nowhere on this. That's when I spoke up. "It seems to me that this entire discussion is being held back by concerns that have not been voiced. Perhaps it's an oversight on my part, and I'm sorry if I've missed something. Until we get those concerns out on the table, I don't think we're going to make progress."

Sonya followed up without hesitation. "My new friend, Paul, has brought up a key issue. It's very important to our company to adopt the ideas and processes that the HP team developed. I'd like to know what's troubling the members of this team and holding us back." She looked at the same staff member and asked her what she thought.

"I just don't know where this fits into my existing priorities," the woman replied. She listed a number of ongoing and anticipated activities that her own team was involved in. "I know this new work is important, but I'm not getting any additional resources, so what am I not supposed to do, in order to do this new work?"

A few other people murmured comments of agreement. Against the greater organization's backdrop of unending pressure, there was real fear of being set up for failure.

Sonya stepped unhesitatingly into the breach. "So let me make clear that it is fine to give up other things in order to move this project forward. Just tell me what you need to give up."

The engineering team leader who had first spoken then explained her ideas for shifting priorities and dropping or delaying certain efforts. Sonya asked a few clarifying questions and then agreed. That broke the logjam. The rest of her staff eagerly came forward with their corresponding ideas, and plans were changed on the spot. Within about 15 minutes of increasingly enthusiastic discussion, the tension was completely broken, and a new, collaborative team had emerged. At the end of the meeting, I was confident that our project would move forward most productively.

Courage of several kinds was displayed in that meeting. It started with the project manager's willingness to take the risk of showing me what was wrong in our own process of engagement with the customer. It continued with Sonya's readiness to hear the unfavorable truth and respond with openness and willingness to confront it head-on. Next was her team's brave response to her request for their trust. Through those back-to-back acts of courage, each one building on the previous one and setting up the next one, we all shared a fine breakthrough and accelerated our work together. *Courage offered in kindness can be contagious.*

But there are times when courage demands something a bit different.

Showing your Claws

Sometimes toughness is warranted, but seldom does it have to be shown in a brutal way. And I always think of it as a last resort. The image I keep is of a lion's paw, with the claws retracted for the moment.

At one of the satellite factories, and I cannot remember which, one of my consulting team members and I were seated at a grey metal table in a small, windowless conference room, facing the door. On the other side of the table was one chair, which had just been vacated by an employee of the client at the conclusion of a 45-minute interview. This was standard process for us, as we collected information on what employees believed to be the client organization's goals, the factors that were critical to success in achieving those goals, the obstacles that were in the way of success, and the potential implications of not overcoming those obstacles. It was our way of gaining a comprehensive picture of the client's business situation and technical needs, when coupled with our direct observations and modeling of the client's factory operations.

My colleague and I prepared for the next interview, scheduled in a few minutes. This would be with a systems engineering team leader named Tom.

The door opened, and a tall man, approaching 40 years of age in my estimation, entered the room. He did not sit down but introduced himself. My teammate and I stood to shake hands, but Tom said, "I know why you're here. You're here to eliminate jobs, and I'm not going to tell you anything."

This was certainly a courageous act, as it was based in his apprehension for not only himself, but his team and the larger organization.

My colleague and I sat back down, while he stood. I said, very calmly, "We're here to try to help your company meet its business objectives for reducing the duration and cost of satellite integration and test processes. We would hope that improving efficiency would make your company more competitive, thereby providing opportunities for more work."

Tom stood, impassive, with his arms crossed in front of his chest.

"I can understand how you feel, Tom, and I would not insist that you help us. However, we were hired by the vice president in charge of this operation to do this work. We do need to speak with systems engineering people, so if you prefer, I can report to him that we did not have your cooperation and would like to have a replacement for our interview."

Tom immediately understood that brief flash of claws. He took a deep breath, exhaled, and uncrossed his arms. Sitting down, he asked, "What do you want to know?"

From that point on, I was careful to treat Tom with the utmost respect. It turned out to be a very productive interview.

Sometime before that interview, I had conducted another at a different company, in which a lack of courage was evident.

The Value of Educating Your Team Members

In 1996, I performed my analysis of integration and test process flow at my very first satellite manufacturing client, Hughes Space and Communications. I was discussing the results with a test supervisor, who was complaining that he was losing good technicians to his competitors. Although I knew the situation well, I asked several questions about the work environment, so as to help this manager discover his own answers.

"Why do you think they leave?"

"The other guys offer them more money."

"Do you think that's the only thing they're after?"

"I don't think they're very happy here. There are a lot of frustrations with how things work in the factory."

"What do you think is most frustrating?"

"Well, mostly I think it's that they end up doing the same things over and over, because of failures and procedural errors. They end up waiting on the engineers to make decisions."

"Could they be educated to make more decisions for themselves?"

"We couldn't afford to educate them."

"Why not?"

"Because if they were better educated, we'd lose them to other companies."

Back to square one. He wasn't going to get to any answer on his own.

"That's already happening. From my own experience, if your technicians were better educated, they'd enjoy the job more and be more likely to stay, and they'd relieve your engineers of a lot of work that the engineers don't like doing."

"Well, we just can't afford to educate them."

"I'm sorry, but I think you can't afford not to."

He didn't buy it. It would have taken a great deal of courage to do so.

Focusing Outward as Well as Inward

In multiple situations during my career and volunteer work, I've been faced with teams that were historically focused inward. Usually, that focus was based on the ways in which the members felt unappreciated or abused, or how they disagreed among themselves. One of the strategies that I've found useful in overcoming the causes of these problems and getting the team focused on improving its performance is to emphasize goals that are based outside the group.

For example, we've discussed the magnetics group that was terribly demoralized at the beginning. While working to let the team know that I was paying attention to their concerns, I also put considerable attention into talking about our customers and what they needed from us. This attention was formalized in the balance of internal and external business metrics that we discussed earlier.

I thought of this approach as raising the team's view from the obstacles in their immediate path to the horizon. It was part of creating a positive vision of the future. As this thinking took hold among the team members, the immediate obstacles gradually took on less importance in their discussions.

I believe that this new focus was a sign of courage, reflecting a gradual increase in the team's confidence that the immediate obstacles would be removed. I also believe that this effect was, to some degree, self-fulfilling. As the team's attention turned to making their customers successful, they just worried less about the minor distractions from that goal.

Much later, I learned from members of the team that they viewed my own confidence in them as an act of courage. I hadn't thought of it that way, but it makes sense. I had plenty of confidence that these people could make the changes they needed to, and so it didn't feel brave to show them the horizon. But from where they stood, discouraged for so long, it looked like a huge, uphill climb that could easily fail. So what they perceived behind my trust in them was courage.

Encouragement, the fostering of courage, is a process that can be self-reinforcing. Focusing the team outward to the horizon, rather than tolerating an isolationist mindset on the nearby obstacles, is a valuable strategy in this process. And it is a two-way process, as I learned.

In a broader sense, this is not just a matter of courage. It is a matter of understanding the dynamics of organizations and interpersonal relationships. It can also be a matter of acting upon empathy or compassion. Whether we're discussing how to make a business successful or how to act as a nation in a community of nations, the evidence I've gathered suggests that focusing outward is a strategy for growing one's own capability and strength. Conversely, I believe it might be argued that isolationism is a recipe for diminishing one's own capability and strength.

There is another way to focus outward and inward at the same time, and that is in leading in such a way as to incorporate, benefit from and encourage diversity in your workforce.

Normalizing Diversity

Diversity in the workforce is a topic that is so extensive that we cannot possibly hope to discuss it adequately here. My purpose, rather, is to convey some pertinent experiences and observations, along with my thoughts on how they relate to the fundamental qualities of leadership.

Around 1989, sometime after I joined HP's Microwave Technology Division, I was making progress toward the goals that my manager, Mr. Joe Lang, had set for me, and I was feeling increasingly confident about achieving that success. We were talking at his desk, when he glanced out the window, spotted someone walking across the courtyard outside, and said, "Oh, there's Andrea."

I said, "Who's Andrea?"

"Andrea used to be Andrew," he said, and explained that she worked in the division located in the building across the courtyard. "Andrew suddenly announced to his group last week that he was becoming Andrea, and now he wears women's clothes."

"Oh," I replied. This was my first experience with an open transgender change in the workplace. "How is that going?" I asked. I was truly curious.

"I hear that it's not going well at all in that group." Joe went into some more detail, including the fact that there were angry arguments over which restroom Andrea would be allowed to use, and more. Suffice it to say, Andrea's team was not being supportive.

It was a basic tenet of the HP Way in those times to accept and welcome human diversity. Our divisions in Sonoma County were no exception. But open gender transition was quite unusual in the workplace then, and I would say that it pushed the limits of the general culture a bit, even in our relatively socially progressive locale.

"Wow," I said at the end of the conversation, "that would be a really interesting management challenge." I meant this sincerely. I had no sense of judgment about Andrea's decision. My thoughts were focused on how I would handle such a situation, in order to support the success and growth of the team.

It came as no surprise, a week or two later, to hear that Andrea was seeking a new job in a different team. But in the wake of my earlier reaction, I must admit to a sense of providential challenge when I learned that Andrea had applied for a production operator job opening in my own group. I smiled when I heard that news. *Well,* I thought, *I asked for it!*

The specific group that had the job opening was comprised of individuals who already demonstrated great openness and compassion for human diversity. That team's supervisor, a woman named Ms. Marti Scott, was a person whose leadership exemplified the best of that tradition. She and I shared similar views on diversity for its own sake and for the purpose of strengthening our teams.

Marti's reaction to Andrea's application for the job was like mine. She was open to the management challenge and even eager to see it through. It was easy for me to give her the support and encouragement she needed in this matter. Moreover, Joe shared similar views. The three of us each understood that striving for the success of our business and doing the right things in regard to diversity were mutually reinforcing imperatives. So, Joe's support enabled me to pursue my approach, and my support enabled Marti to pursue hers. It was never a question among us that this was the right thing to do.

Marti's team welcomed Andrea into the team's job interview process, among other candidates. As the interviews proceeded, it became clear that she was the leading candidate. Marti reported to me that her team had already agreed that, should Andrea join the team, she would be allowed to use the women's restroom. And all other necessary accommodations had already been decided, including how the team would communicate with other teams about all this.

The upshot was that the team was focused on the knowledge, skills and commitment that Andrea would bring to the team, how she would perform in the job, and how best to help her be successful. This focus was fundamentally no different than it would have been with any other candidate, although the special circumstances added a bit of complexity. I was quite proud, though not surprised, at their way of addressing this challenge as a team, and their maturity in reaching their decisions and making their plans. It was courageous.

Andrea did win the job, and along with the rest of the team, I gave her a normal welcome into the group. I would not be honest if I didn't admit that it felt a bit odd, at first, to know that the person facing me as a woman wasn't physically a woman. But as time went by, and it was clear that she was focused on her success in the job, her gender identity became less and less a distinguishing feature of her presence.

Several months after joining us, Andrea came to see me about some minor matter related to production, which we discussed across the table in my office. As we finished that up, I asked, "Do you have a bit more time to spend with me?"

"Sure."

"I'd like to know how you're doing. I mean, how are you feeling about things here?"

Andrea leaned forward in her chair. "You know, Paul, I am happy for the first time in a long time. There are whole days that go by that I don't even think about it. It's just not an issue."

"I'm very glad to hear that, Andrea. If you ever feel the need to talk with me, please don't hesitate."

Andrea's observation that she was able to put her own situation out of her mind, for even a day, was a very gratifying testament to the qualities of our team and the principles on which we tried to operate. Her courage had been met by equal courage, as well as compassion, from the rest of our team. It was one of those moments that left me celebrating internally.

This was not the end of the story, though. Andrea gradually suffered increasing emotional difficulties that I understood to be unrelated to her job, and despite the team's continuing support, she left the company several months later. I was disappointed, and perhaps a bit more so than I would have been at the loss of any other capable employee. Andrea's presence had been a constant reminder of the fine qualities of our team and, thereby, a source of strength for it.

This was a particularly vivid lesson in diversity in the workforce, but not my first. The 1970s had been a time of upheaval in workplaces dominated by male managers and male professionals. Caltech itself admitted its first female undergraduates in 1970, my junior year, although there were female graduate students long before that. I saw very few women in professional positions in either the aerospace or the utility industry. By the 1980s, when I moved from the utility industry into the electronics industry, we began to see more women among the professions, but still a small minority. It was a very difficult time for them.

In engineering hiring processes, I tried particularly to hire qualified women. As I observed in my teams and others, their presence added a dimension to discussion and decision-making processes that simply seemed out of reach before that. Of course, my experience in this regard isn't unusual at all, and the relative effectiveness of mixed-gender teams has been well-documented elsewhere. In my view, the sort of experience we had with Andrea simply added another factor to the calculus of gender diversity, and I believe that this has been validated by others over time.

I have always been a believer that cultural diversity is an equally powerful tool for improving the effectiveness of teams, when the members are able to tap that value. To my way of thinking, this incorporates ethnic and "racial" (if you'll forgive the term) differences, as well as people with various physical and mental disabilities.

Diversity deserves to become the norm in the workplace. It is a source of strength, resilience, and creativity.

Where have I felt less than successful in this? Two areas come to mind.

The first would be in not having sufficient success in hiring black employees into the organizations that I've run. I wish I had the chance to do that over, because that would be a worthy challenge to overcome.

The second area would be in the promotion of women and minorities into leadership positions. A good fraction of the supervisors and managers in my organizations have been women, and C8 MediSensors had two female vice presidents, although they were outnumbered by males. I am glad to be able to say that a number of senior leaders who have worked in my organizations were gay or lesbian. Still, considering the many leaders who have worked in my organizations, few were members of ethnic or "racial" minorities or had significant physical disabilities, and that is sad. Increasing the representation of these groups in leadership positions is another worthy challenge, and again, I would wish to have been a better contributor to that.

I believe that one who does nothing to support those goals commits, thereby, an act equivalent to hidden bias. Such an act of omission is camouflaged and difficult even to recognize before it can be confronted. In this respect, such an act of omission is more insidious than overt bias or prejudice, which can be recognized and confronted immediately. Perhaps this is why the problem continues. It's just so easy to hide from the problem, or to let other matters take priority, rather than to do what's necessary to strip the camouflage away and address the bias openly.

And addressing diversity is not just about wanting to do right by people, or about having the courage to do so. This is not just about the Tin Man and the Cowardly Lion. What is the Scarecrow's role in this aspect of leadership? His role is partly about understanding the mechanics of managing diversity, but more importantly, it's about understanding the economics of business. Women and the minorities constitute the majority of our population in America. Our economy simply can't afford to have less than the maximum contribution from each of these groups, and that means as consumers, as workers, and as leaders. We need to utilize the best talent we can find to achieve the best economic growth and resilience that our society can create.

In regard to diversity, I am pleased in my retirement to be making a small contribution on the local front, as a member of the board of directors of the Career Technical Education Foundation Sonoma County.[10] This is an organization that has created a successful public-private model for investing in educational programs within our middle schools, high schools, and local community college to help our very diverse student population to become exposed to career paths that can excite them, and to give them a start in those directions. While there is much to do, there is much progress that might be emulated elsewhere.

Maintaining True North: The Value of Management by Walking Around

How can leaders achieve the best results in organizational alignment and action? How can they engender the courage to define and follow the best courses?

I learned the HP practice of "Management by Walking Around" when I was in my early thirties. This technique has been widely described and discussed, and Dave Packard touched on it briefly in his 1995 book, *The HP Way*,[11] which is his description of his and Bill Hewlett's incomparable corporate leadership style. It seemed an obvious way for leaders to stay in touch with the folks at all levels of the organization, to pick up on problems before they became major, and to give a personal touch to sharing the values of the leadership team. But Management by Walking Around has a much, much more powerful purpose, one that I didn't figure out until I was near the end of my career.

A very common ailment in organizations is what I call "compass drift." When one is interviewing client personnel at all levels of the organization, from CEO to production operator, one cannot help but be struck by the frequent finding that, while the top executives want to steer the company ship in a certain direction, the folks at the bottom of the organization chart are rowing in exactly the opposite direction. Taking the analogy a bit further, it's usually true that the compass heading being used by the people in the organization varies gradually from top to bottom. There isn't usually a stark change somewhere in the middle. So why this gradual drift in heading among the management levels of an organization?

I have experienced compass drift in organizations that I led. I recall speaking with a vice president of C8 MediSensors, explaining some specific results that I wanted from his department. When he replied, he restated those objectives slightly differently, and less stringently. The compass had already drifted in that exchange, and that was only across one level of management and happened in just one moment.

In my consulting work, I frequently was in the position of explaining to a client executive that a certain department or a certain level of the organization was headed ninety or one-hundred-eighty degrees away from his stated objective. It was usually a surprise to the executive and often a great annoyance.

So why does this happen, and how does Management by Walking Around fit in?

Imagine that you are a middle manager in an organization that has been working a particular way toward particular objectives for a long time. Suddenly your boss announces that there will be a new direction. Objectives are changing, and maybe the work will need to be done in different ways.

What goes through your mind, almost without thought? *How will I explain this to my team?* you wonder. *They won't react well. How can I soften the blow? How can I minimize the perceived change?*

So, when announcing the changes to your team, you modify the message a bit. You don't think you're really affecting the nature of the changes. Surely it can't hurt to state it a different way, and maybe adjust when and how the details of the changes will be implemented. After all, you don't expect your boss to be aware of all the mitigating factors in your department.

The result is that you've changed the ordered heading by a few degrees, or maybe several degrees.

And then, if the people reporting to you are, say, first-level managers, they go through the same kind of thought process. And when they communicate the changes to their teams, the heading changes some more, even from what you planned.

One way to look at this is that leadership is a political process. A leader must win the support of constituents. Granted, this is usually easier in a hierarchical organization than in a public political campaign, because employment relationships create position power for the leaders, but it is still a process that needs attention and action. Managers are always negotiating objectives and the means for achieving them. That process is ongoing, up and down the organization. This negotiation can be a sign of courage, but only in certain cases where defiance to objectives is being demonstrated, revealing severe organizational dysfunction. More often, I have seen such negotiation reveal a lack of courage, an unwillingness to pass a difficult message on to one's subordinates in the organization.

As a member of the last generation of managers in HP to actually see David Packard and Bill Hewlett while they ran the company, I greatly appreciated their commitment to visit informally with people at all levels of the organization and to talk about virtually any topic of importance to the company. These were opportunities for them to transmit their leadership style to new generations of employees, while keeping their fingers on the pulse of the organization.

What I didn't understand explicitly until later was the fact that these visits accomplished an even more important role. By discussing company objectives and directions with employees, Bill and Dave short-circuited much of the management negotiating in between. When Bill or Dave said, "We're going north," figuratively speaking, no one argued. People might ask questions and even advocate different ideas, but when the decision was clearly the decision, that was the end of the discussion. So any manager located in between Bill or Dave and the person they'd been talking with would be foolish to advocate any different direction. (It has occurred to me that some of Bill's and Dave's destinations for walking around may not have been chosen randomly at all, but rather were selected to counter specific compass drift.)

Management by Walking Around is a political communication process, and a very effective one. I think I must have understood this subliminally when I explained to the corporate vice president, as I related at the beginning of this book, that he ought to have informal lunches with people in his organization. But I hadn't yet consciously recognized the link to compass drift and the political process at work.

Later on, I learned to use a code phrase with my team to mitigate the tendency toward negotiation: When I stated a new objective or reinforced an existing one, I would say, "This is true north." Still, it wasn't always easy to maintain that heading.

Now, as an exercise in courage, if you are a first-line supervisor or a middle manager and are told of a change in direction at work, you might consider testing the message via an informal discussion with a higher-level manager. If you detect a difference in compass heading, then you might go further up the chain. It's risky, of course, because the managers in between may take offense. Or you may become a hero.

As CEO of C8 MediSensors, I always particularly valued the few employees who would stop by my office to ask business questions and test the messages that they were hearing. I made sure to keep those lines of communications open, because they provided me with a way to test the messaging up and down the organization. I always kept those conversations in confidence, unless the employee and I agreed on a different course in a particular case. Naturally, I always tested the employee's intentions the first time or two, because the last thing I wanted was to encourage selfish "tattling" or other nefarious activity. As it happened, I never detected such, but only sincere desire to keep the company moving forward and the courage to keep seeking better ways. We were blessed, by and large, with a great group of employees.

This discussion is not meant to diminish the importance of encouraging constructive challenges. It is just as important to value those people who are willing to disagree with a policy, a decision, or a process in a sincere, knowledgeable, constructive way. If executives don't pay sincere attention to those challenges, they will be prone to ignoring dangers to the organization's success. The leader must remain sensitive to the balance of constructive contention and determined intention.

What other lessons might we learn about leading an organization through times of chaotic, dangerous change?

Leadership through the Storm

In the mid-1980s, the global market for microwave and radio frequency communications test equipment changed dramatically. HP's dominant position was suddenly threatened by competitors who were nimble and unafraid to copy HP products and produce them less expensively. Sales growth was down, and HP was losing market share, in the context of a generally slowing market.

The affected HP divisions reacted as many companies did in that time period. We were subjected to outsourcing and downsizing. These were traumatic times, and I observed HP's leaders closely to see how they would act in these circumstances. Would their leadership styles change? If so, how would their teams react?

As it happened, in my opinion, our own division manager showed dramatic, unexpected changes in style. From my vantage point several layers down the organization, he seemed to become harsher, less forgiving, even less friendly. No doubt he bore a terrible burden, much as I would decades later. But there was no doubt in my mind that his leadership style had changed. As it happened, I believed the change was permanent.

In the midst of this turmoil, I had a conversation with our quality manager, who reported to the division manager. He was a retired Navy officer, so I couched my discussion in nautical terms.

"Suppose you're the captain of a ship," I said, "with a particular style of commanding the crew. But now the ship enters a terrible storm. Will you change your command style in the middle of the storm?"

"Good question," he said. "In my experience, that's not what happens."

"Right. Because if it did, then the crew might be led into uncertainty about their captain, right in the middle of the storm. They might be distracted from doing what's necessary to save the ship."

"Exactly," he replied.

"And even more, when the ship gets out of the storm, will the captain change command style back to the old one? The crew might be even more uncertain about that."

"Good point."

"So my view would be, the captain should maintain his command style in the storm but practice his style more intensively. More orders, quicker, maybe. But not a different style."

"That's what I like about being a manager," he replied. "You learn something every day."

He missed my point, I think, about our division manager. Or he didn't want to pursue it. Or he lacked the courage to do so. Or perhaps he believed I was wrong about our division manager's style. Nevertheless, my way of thinking about leadership through the storm stayed with me.

But when I think about this with the benefit of many more years' experience, I am inclined to soften this view a bit. I recall a later incident at HP, when I was still an inexperienced manager, and Marti Scott, she of the excellent work in building diversity in her work group, expressed a concern with my own variable style in the face of changing circumstances. "When something happens," she said, "the people don't know which Paul is going to show up." Now I understand that the problem wasn't that my style changed, but that it changed in unpredictable ways.

Plenty has been written about the need to be flexible in one's communication style, whether in a leadership position or not. I think that what seemed so stark a change in that division manager's style, so long ago, was only because it may have been very different from what we had experienced from him before that point. So perhaps what is important for the ship's captain is to be predictable. The crew members will have an easier time maintaining their confidence in the leader if they see the captain that they expect in any particular circumstance.

Many years later, during the crisis at C8 MediSensors, I resolved to be myself and to practice my leadership style as intensively as necessary to get through the storm. I found that it wasn't always easy to maintain that style under the pressure. And I think that what I really did was to vary my style within relatively small limits. No great excursions. I think this kept us on an even keel.

And so, with all these lessons at our backs, we are brought to the questions of what courage is and how it manifests in leadership and organizations.

What is Courage? What is Not Courage?

Countless philosophers, traceable back at least to Plato, have attempted to define *courage*. Some of these took humanistic views, others religious. Often these definitions were made only in reference to other virtues. Taken together, these philosophical discussions over thousands of years paint a picture of courage, but it remains one burdened by blurry lines and indistinct colors.

A casual look at a dictionary reveals fascinating imprecision in the definition of *courage*. Often one sees circular definitions, in which such terms as *courage*, *bravery*, *boldness* or *valor* refer to each other.

One can find *courage* defined as the willingness to act in the face of risk to oneself, without fear. But if there is no fear, is there courage? I would rather think of courage as the willingness to act despite fear. In that sense, *courage* is not *fearlessness*, which is sometimes defined as the trait of feeling no fear or, alternatively, showing no fear. One might show fear and still act courageously.

Most definitions at least imply that the contemplated action is in favor of a greater good, so that some form of selflessness is involved, but not always. So courage is a variable quality that depends on the context.

It would seem that these concepts are best learned from experience and context, rather than from book definitions.

After beginning the drafting of this book, I found that only a handful of books has been published in the attempt to analyze and teach courage as an element of organizational leadership. The best may be *First Person: Tales of Management Courage and Tenacity*,[12] edited by Thomas Teal, which consists of a dozen stories of courageous business leadership that were first published in the 1980s and '90s by Harvard Business Review. It's telling that the book is out of print.

Most of these books are written by consultants who have quite limited direct experience as managers. Most provide coaching in interpersonal communications, and a few address right-and-wrong ethical decision-making. Some extrapolate characteristics of "moral courage" based on experiences with "physical courage," such as in the sport of boxing. None span the scale from first-level supervision to executive management. None do an adequate job of defining the various forms of courage that people exhibit. Even the great Peter F. Drucker wrote in 1963 article that, "Unfortunately I know of no procedure or checklist for managerial courage."[13]

Interestingly, many biographical books about well-known business leaders exhibit an undertone of courage, or a lack thereof, but never explicitly discuss courage or analyze its characteristics. For example, the recently-published *Steve Jobs*,[14] about the late co-founder of Apple, and *Jack: Straight from the Gut*,[15] about Jack Welch, the legendary head of General Electric, provide descriptions of myriad interactions of these business leaders with other leaders, but the word courage seems never to appear in those stories. The word is never mentioned in *The HP Way*. Certainly the presence or absence of courage is implied in many of these stories. It's just not discussed explicitly.

My sampling of various similar books about business leaders, although certainly not exhaustive, reveals a similar void. Perhaps there are books on particular business leaders that do mention the word courage, but it seems curious that it would not be nearly ubiquitous.

Indeed, it seems a shame that there is not a book on courage in business leadership that is the equivalent of John F. Kennedy's *Profiles in Courage*,[16] which is exclusively about particularly courageous US Senators of the past. Teal's book, mentioned above, seems to be as close as they get, but it does not share the style, popularity or panache of Kennedy's.

An Internet search easily reveals numerous websites and blogs devoted to the teaching of courage, and a few are aimed at leaders. I have found none that seems authoritative in the sense of having a solid analytical base. Many of them categorize types of courage, but there is no accepted number of categories. Some cite three types of courage, others four, five or six. In that respect, the teaching of courage becomes less a transmission of knowledge and more a promulgation of belief. I think that, as a whole, this body of work remains unsatisfactory as a source for learning by leaders at any organizational level.

But we have to have somewhere to start. I happen to believe that a useful categorization of types of courage includes these six, which I have adapted from a particular website[17] but can be found elsewhere:

- Moral – doing the "right" thing, despite a risk of opposition or loss of status
- Intellectual – opening oneself to ideas that differ from one's own opinions
- Emotional – opening oneself to unpleasant emotions
- Social – standing up for oneself or others despite the risk of alienating others
- Spiritual – facing up to the uncertainty of the purpose for one's existence
- Physical – facing a challenge involving the risk of physical injury or death

It seems clear that the first four categories are those that most often are involved in business leadership. Leaders can fail at any of these, but from my experience, the most challenging situations are those that call for moral courage.

It may be asked, before we proceed, whether there are multiple types of courage or, rather, just one kind of courage that manifests differently in different situations. Well, that's certainly a different way of looking at it that may be valid. But in the end, for our purposes, I think it doesn't matter very much which of those two models we choose. I'll leave that debate to others. The analytical model described above will serve us here with sufficient clarity.

Considering the idea of moral courage, choosing the "right" thing can often be difficult. Is it the right thing in regard to complying with social norms, or the right thing for complying with the law, or the right thing for maximizing profits or sales or some other business metric? Is it the right thing for oneself or one's organization or nation? What is "right?" Didn't we all learn everything we needed to know in kindergarten? Not exactly. Training in ethics is designed to help people recognize these situations and choose the right thing.

Newly minted in my first supervisory job at HP, I was confronted with a small moral dilemma. An employee had come to me with a serious personal problem that required me to make a decision on whether to help him, which would cost the company some money, or not to help. I felt that the "right" thing would be to help the employee, because it felt ethically proper, would maintain a mutually respectful relationship with this employee, and would have seemed equally just if another typical employee were in the same position. Just to test my new environment, I took the question to my manager and asked what he would want me to do. His reply was perfect: "Do the right thing." I never felt that I had to ask that kind of question again. My manager had clearly shown that he trusted me to exert proper judgment on such matters. This may not be a satisfying example for everyone, because the judgments involved may not be quantifiable, and the feelings involved may not be easily explained.

Perhaps it is helpful to note that where moral decisions often go astray is when the decision-maker has trouble distinguishing what's right for himself or herself from what's right for the organization or for the world at large. Think of the days when the king or the queen was the state, and what was good for the king or queen was automatically good for the state.

From my personal experience, it is important to be able to recognize abnormal behavior in regard to courage. I recall working briefly with a consultant whom I found to be unmanageable – oblivious to direction and defiant. I also viewed his results as rather meager and not worthy of his remuneration. As I moved to terminate the relationship, he asserted that his contribution was "unprecedented and game-changing." I replied that only his insubordination was unprecedented in my experience. That only made him angrier.

I later learned from a psychologist, to whom I described this behavior, that the consultant likely suffered from what is currently called "narcissistic personality disorder." From my description, the psychologist further described the consultant as having "borderline tendencies." He cautioned me, "You do not want to provoke this person." What might have appeared as courage on this consultant's part, if one didn't know him well, was actually recklessness, based on his personal conviction that he could not fail at anything or even make a mistake. Recklessness is, perhaps, courage gone pathologically wild.

Let's examine some of the stories of people and situations related in this book, to see what kind of courage, or lack thereof, was displayed.

The aerospace company vice president who lost his position shortly after I met him (see "A Look behind the Curtain") not only lacked the knowledge to succeed at his job, he seemed to lack the ability to face the difficult emotions that were necessary for him to master. And he lacked the will to do the right thing. So I believe that his failings manifested as a lack of moral and emotional courage in that moment. I had only a two-hour snapshot of the man, and I have no idea what personal or other pressures he was under, so I would not presume to stand in judgment of him as a person. Yet, his professional position was high enough to brook no excuses, because his failings in that moment adversely affected many people's futures and his entire company's fortunes.

The executives at Raytheon Missile Systems (see "Product Development and Business Risk") showed great intellectual and emotional courage by inviting me to hold up a mirror that showed them the dysfunction in their organization. Perhaps they also demonstrated moral courage by accepting what needed to be done and proceeding, rather than sticking with the status quo.

Furthermore, recalling that same case, no new product development goes perfectly smoothly. Leading a new product development through a series of checkpoints requires a great deal of intellectual and social courage on the part of all participants. Moral and emotional courage may also be called upon. People's ideas and positions are constantly at risk, and making it successfully through the process draws on everyone's courage.

The managers and engineers that I worked with in the gas turbine power generation businesses of GE and Westinghouse (see "Product Development and the Customer") showed intellectual and social courage by accepting the idea that they needed to hear directly from customers before moving ahead with new products. They showed moral courage in moving ahead on the basis of the new information they'd gleaned. I was not present when they had to discuss with their managers their intentions to seek input from customers, nor did I know what their managers had to say when confronted with the new information. I can only imagine that those were difficult meetings, in which prevailing beliefs were overturned.

The HP managers (see "World Class Manufacturing and Beyond: At Last, Someone Cares") who immediately approved my proposal to clean up the magnetics area and to perform health monitoring for the team members demonstrated a high degree of moral courage. The women who volunteered to learn the crystal growth process demonstrated social, emotional and even physical courage. And their supervisor, who was ultimately transferred to another position, showed great moral, intellectual, emotional and social courage throughout his efforts to improve his performance, and that's why I supported him for as long as I did.

I think that similar types of courage were exhibited by the people at TRW Space Systems (see "What Will You Do When It Breaks?") during my initial consultancy. They had to face up to great challenges

162

to their existing beliefs, their plans and even aspects of their corporate culture. Later on, when we began implementing solutions, the same kinds of courage were demonstrated by the new leader's team and members of my consulting team (see "Naming the Fear is the First Step"). That collaborative process could have broken down at several points, and it was a combination of pure moral, intellectual, emotional and social courage that made us successful together.

The assembly shift supervisor at Space Systems/Loral (see "A Leader is a Teacher"), who struggled with a moral dilemma about leaving or staying to help her team, demonstrated a great deal of emotional, social and moral courage, in my opinion. There was also an element of intellectual courage, as she considered the new thought that in her management position, as a leader, she ought to consider herself a teacher.

At NEC America (see "Listen When the Heart Has an Insight"), from the general manager to the engineers, the staff showed great intellectual, social and emotional courage to accept and make the changes necessary to meet their business goals. There was an important element of moral courage as well, which compelled them to do the right thing by their people at the same time. It was an elegant solution of great integrity.

The satellite systems engineering team leader (see "Showing your Claws") who initially refused to participate in my consulting interview process showed something of social and, perhaps, moral courage. He thought he was doing the right thing by standing up for himself and others. I'm afraid that I resorted to a form of coercion to secure his cooperation, by suggesting that I would report his intransigence to his management. His decision to cooperate did not diminish his courage. But I hoped that if I carefully showed him respect in the subsequent interview, he would respond with the emotional and intellectual courage to change his attitude, and so he did.

The satellite test supervisor (see "The Value of Educating Your Team Members") who would not acknowledge the value of educating his technicians might have thought that he was showing courage in holding the line, but I would contend that he showed a lack of intellectual courage, at least, by closing his mind.

Recall our story related in "Leadership through the Storm." Whether one is a first-line supervisor or the CEO of a vast corporation, maintaining a reliable leadership style is fundamental to encouraging one's team members. In a crisis, this need for a large degree of steadfastness may challenge the leaders' moral, intellectual, emotional and social courage. And there is always a crisis at hand, whether major or minor. This is one reason I think that courage is perhaps the most fundamental quality of a leader.

Lastly, deciding on the proper course for the organization is an act of courage in every sense. Maintaining that direction despite the constant tendency of the organizational compass to drift requires a sustained, broadly courageous effort by leaders up and down the organization. *For the leader, it is essential in every situation to have a grasp of the type of courage that is being asked of each person, and to weigh each person's capacity in that moment to offer up that very courage.*

With this understanding in hand, we turn to Dorothy to further our quest.

DOROTHY

"If you were really great and powerful, you'd keep your promises!"
– Dorothy

She is young and naïve to the ways of the world, but she wants to learn and to expand her horizons. She does not know that she is about to embark on a quest that will lead her to understanding. How will she apply this understanding to her mission and to her life?

It seems to me that finding a way home is not Dorothy's real goal. Her quest is much greater than that. She seeks understanding. She is, above all, a student. We might say that her course of study is leadership. In this context, it would seem that Glinda serves as her instructor, leading Dorothy down the path of learning but not giving her the answer until there is no alternative.

What are the key lessons that Dorothy learns? I think the first three are these:

- ***Knowledge and wisdom may be found in the most unexpected places.*** Get to know the people you work with, and show them that you will never underestimate them.

- *Love and compassion are the qualities that properly bind us together.* They must be nurtured, and they must not be left behind.

- *Courage can emerge even among the meekest, if their cause demands it.* Seek and liberate the inner strength of each person, starting with yourself.

Having reached this point, it is entirely proper to ask how these three lessons might apply to people serving in different kinds of business leadership or individual contributor positions, whether those be in a large organization or a small business. You must explore this landscape for yourself, but Dorothy can offer some general landmarks. That guidance is presented in Appendix B: Dorothy's Travel Guide to the Yellow Brick Road. Perhaps you will find that the answers are not so different among those various roles.

There is yet one more lesson that Dorothy learns, but it does not reveal itself until the very end of her journey. It is the most difficult lesson for her to perceive, for it requires her to see the Wizard for what he truly is.

So, at last, we are ready to proceed to the end of our quest, where we will confront the Wizard himself.

THE WIZARD

"I'm a very good man. I'm just a very bad Wizard."
— The Wizard of Oz

At their first meeting, the Wizard sends Dorothy and her companions on yet another quest, one that he believes will kill them and relieve him of responsibility. But they succeed and return, only to find in the end that he is just a bumbling old man hiding behind a curtain, projecting an illusion of power. So he bestows mere symbols of what Dorothy's companions already possess, their knowledge and wisdom, love and compassion, and courage. He cannot bring Dorothy to her goal. It falls to Glinda, the Good Witch, to show Dorothy that she had the means to reach her goal all along.

I choose to think of the Wizard as representing hope. But he is an evasive, capricious kind of hope. As soon as that hope has been realized, it slips away, first when the Wizard demands that Dorothy and her friends destroy the Wicked Witch of the West, and again later, when he admits to his fraud and then proves unable to help Dorothy return home. He is a paradox, at once offering hope but dispensing only disappointment.

Leadership is its own paradox. It's best done by demanding the best from everyone and not letting any important issue go

167

unmanaged. But it's best fulfilled by giving up control to get control.

A leader's Yellow Brick Road starts with the understanding that there is no problem in an organization that is not a leadership problem. By this, I mean that at bottom, every problem is caused by something that the leaders do or don't do. If you're the leader, don't ever blame the folks for what goes wrong. Take the blame yourself, and then fix the root cause. The hard part is following the trail far enough to understand the root cause, which will always come back to you. Fixing it elegantly, by the application of knowledge, wisdom, love, compassion and courage, is leadership.

Great organizations share among their members a common vision of the future that they'll create, based on a common set of fundamental values. They share the specific goals that will realize that vision. And they are designed to implement a strategy that plays to their strengths and renders their weaknesses irrelevant to achieving those goals and that vision. A great leader is one who sees that these visions, values, goals and strategies are adopted by the organization and that they are implemented with knowledge, wisdom, love, compassion and courage in the face of every adversity.

When I consider great leaders in history, I have come to ask, "Did that person have a solid mix of knowledge, wisdom, love, compassion and courage?" In every case I have considered, I have found flaws. So being a great leader doesn't require flawlessness. But great leaders tend to show a good helping of most of those qualities, while poor leaders seem to uniformly exhibit gaping voids in more than one of those qualities. See if you agree about the leaders that you admire and those you dislike. And remember that no leader is born with all those qualities. They emerge over time as the person develops, or they don't. Some historical figures who turned out to be great leaders did not show such promise when they were young.

Fiction has the great advantage over reality that the leaders in stories can be endowed with huge amounts of any or all of those qualities. Perhaps you have your own favorites. I think first of Cyrano de Bergerac, my favorite fictional hero, who is brilliant, witty, unquestionably courageous, compassionate to a fault, and deeply, hopelessly in love. His unbending spirit inspires all around him to either love him or, if they are enemies, to despise him. I think next of Don Quixote, adorably mad, but knowledgeable, loving and insanely courageous. Then there's Jean Valjean of "Les Miserables," who never fails to show all those qualities of leadership.

These are three beloved fictional characters. Why are they so beloved? None of them leads a great organization. They all die at the end of their long struggles. Yet, each in his own way achieves his goal and leaves behind an unsullied integrity of spirit, an unbroken combination of selfless leadership qualities that we cannot help but admire.

We are real people, with real flaws. We each follow our own Yellow Brick Road toward some distant, glowing destination. And we must live with our flaws and try to improve, as we struggle along the way. Our improvement comes through the influence of the people and things we find and of what we learn as we go. And all the while, we must retain our hope.

Dorothy, near the end of her story, said that to find what she truly wanted, she needed to look no further than her own home. Better never to have left Kansas, it would seem. Does this mean that she had forgotten the three lessons about knowledge and wisdom, love and compassion, and courage, and how central these qualities are to effective leadership?

No, there is another way to look at it.

I promised earlier to tell you Dorothy's fourth lesson in leadership. We can hear this lesson in Dorothy's final words after her return from Oz, if we but listen closely enough. To do so, we must take a broader perspective, as we have about Dorothy's entire story, because this final lesson is not just about leadership. It is also about life, and about what exactly *home* means. And it is precisely the same final lesson that I discovered at the end of my own Yellow Brick Road:

- ***The hope that we seek may prove evasive and capricious.*** What we find along the way – the strengths and abilities that we discover we have, the tools that we learn to use, and the friends that we make – are the more reliable destination.

In other words, there's no place like home.

ACKNOWLEDGMENTS

It would take another book to thank all the people who taught me over a career that spanned 43 years and a quest that began when I was just a boy. That book would include those I love, those I like, and even those I cannot abide. But here, I wish to thank the following people for the gifts of knowledge, wisdom, love, compassion and courage that they each imparted.

First, my family. For 45 years, I have counted on my wife, Michelle, to hold steady to true north through every storm, and she has never failed me in any attribute of leadership. Our children, Sam, Beth and Josh, have taught me the deeper meaning of wisdom, mostly by wryly forcing me to figure out my mistakes. My late parents, Joseph L. and Adele Zygielbaum, taught me especially of courage. Michelle's late parents, Arthur and Helen Margolese, were like second parents to me and carried on those lessons and more. And my brother, Art, showed me the love of knowledge from an early age. My extended family has provided additional coursework.

Professor Richard Dean, retired from Caltech, saw that I was a worthy candidate for admission as a student, helped me adjust to life there and, much later in life, pointed out what I'd gained from that education. The late Professor Rolf Sabersky extended kindness and friendship as I figured out how to navigate my difficult curriculum, and he saw fit to sponsor my master's year at Caltech.

Dr. David G. Elliot, Lance Hays, and the entire Liquid Metal MHD group in JPL's Propulsion Division, took me on as a technician in 1970 and gave me the beginnings of my career in technology.

The late Dr. Vance Cooper and Al Dolbec, who were my supervisors at EPRI, guided me through my first management experiences, and Jack Guy taught me some of the ropes in Washington. The late Sy Alpert, Jerry Weiss, and Mario Rabinowitz were three of my fellows at EPRI whose experience was a wellspring of wisdom.

The late Dr. William E. Shoupp, Vice President of Research and Development, Westinghouse Electric Company, befriended me while I was managing research programs for EPRI. We had several opportunities to share long car rides to remote sites, and I was enthralled by his experiences in management and life. Bill told me once that I'd never retire, but he did not foresee how cancer would change my life, and it's the one time that I found him to be incorrect. Bill himself never did retire.

The late Bill Hewlett and the late David Packard built a brilliant star of a company. It was like post-graduate school for management. I learned a great deal from their examples and from all the people I worked with there over 21 years, including the Component Engineering, Magnetics, Surface Acoustic Wave, and Thin Film groups, and my teammates in HP's and Agilent's Strategic Business Development Organization. I want especially to thank Bill Lawson, Joe Lang, Doug Raymond, Rick Pearson, and my dear friends Larry Rosenfeld, Dana Furia, Larry Pendergrass, Rick Ruthnick, Dr. Scott Elliott and John Lamy.

The late Dr. Eberhard Rechtin was already a role model to me when I was just a nine-year-old with dreams of space and big plans. He remained a mentor through much of my career, although he was hardly aware of that. The memories of what he taught me never left.

In 1974, the late Dr. Joseph W. Pepper was a Stanford PhD candidate working on a project newly under my responsibility as an EPRI project manager. Joe subsequently joined EPRI in a similar position, and he became my role model and daily mentor by virtue of his extraordinary intelligence, leadership qualities and sincere friendship. We lost touch with each other for a long time, but then we regained our acquaintance and friendship, and Joe joined the board of C8 MediSensors when I asked him to. Eventually serving as chairman of the board, he saw us through a difficult end. Joe remained my steadfast friend until his passing in early 2016. I frequently find myself asking, "What would Joe do?"

Dr. Robert P. McNamara and the late Dr. Jan Lipson were my dear friends and co-conspirators at Caltech. The three of us met three nursing students at the same exchange dance with LA County/USC Medical Center's nursing school, and we all married those sweethearts within a few months of each other. Our families remained in close contact for decades, until Jan had the idea for a novel, non-invasive glucose monitor, and he and Mac formed a company and asked for my help. That became the first time we'd worked together formally. It's impossible to catalogue everything that I learned from these two men. When Jan died suddenly in a terrible bicycling accident in 2010, we honored him by redoubling our efforts to bring his invention to market, but not all stories have a happy ending.

Sonya Sepahban took the reins of spacecraft integration and test, as well as systems engineering, at the conclusion of my initial consultancy at TRW Space Systems in 1999. She treated me with

174

great respect and friendship, and I found her to be an extraordinarily talented leader. Her engineering knowledge was deep, and she knew how to apply it effectively in her position. We became friends, to my great pleasure, and have remained in contact over the years, while she climbed the corporate ladders at Northrup Grumman and General Dynamics and then moved on to her great personal calling to encourage and support innovation and entrepreneurialism, especially among young women. When I mentioned my idea for this book to Sonya, she exhorted me to see it through and hasn't stopped since. I am grateful for all of that.

Fred Toney joined C8 MediSensors as CFO in 2010, and besides teaching me about the world of corporate finance, he became a dear friend. Fred supported me fiercely in our effort to make the company successful and demonstrated great leadership qualities throughout that struggle.

It would be an oversight not to acknowledge, at least collectively, all the wonderful consulting clients who invited me into their companies, their personnel who enabled me to provide those services, and my many coworkers at JPL, EPRI, Hewlett Packard, Agilent Technologies, and C8 MediSensors, all of whom cajoled me down that Yellow Brick Road.

Patrice LePera produced the beautiful cover art for this book, and I greatly appreciate how it captures the essence of my message.

Debby Zygielbaum, my niece, led me through the mechanics of publication, and I am grateful for her knowledge, time and patience.

Finally, I thank Sonya Sepahban, the late Joe Pepper, Scott Elliott, John Lamy, Rick Pearson, Larry Pendergrass, Larry Rosenfeld, Fred Toney and Mario Rabinowitz, as well as my wife, Michelle, for giving of their time to review drafts of all or parts of this book. Their honest, insightful feedback was instrumental to its improvement and completion.

I am a most fortunate person to have had all these wonderful people, and many more, in my life.

APPENDIX A:
PRODUCT DEVELOPMENT AS A
RISK-REDUCTION PROCESS

Every organization that develops products has a process, or rather a set of processes, for doing so. Many of these processes include periodic reports and formal reviews, in an effort to gauge progress and examine problem areas, although these methods are becoming somewhat less common nowadays with the ascendance of lean and agile development methods. Still, generally speaking, the larger the organization, the more complex and formal these processes are. Various tools for managing the product life cycle process, or at least for managing product research and development, are available today and can be found under such topics as "Product Development Resources" or "Critical Design Reviews." Donald G. Reinertsen's *The Principles of Product Development Flow: Second Generation Lean Product Development*, mentioned earlier, presents a fine analytical discussion of modern principles.

Hewlett Packard's Test and Measurement business in the 1990s had its Product Life Cycle Process, which spanned every phase, from conception through development, manufacturing, and finally obsolescence. In the middle of that decade, as a member of a team that reviewed, updated and standardized the processes across the company, I had noted some disturbing things about how people viewed this life cycle, and especially the way that the company managed the transitions between phases.

Every phase began and ended with a formal "release" to the next phase. This release involved a review of various factors in the development, and specific criteria that were to be met before release to the next phase. Did the product design meet manufacturability standards? Did product samples pass their reliability tests satisfactorily? Were the manufacturing processes statistically capable of producing products that all performed within their specifications? Were the marketing and support plans on track? It all added up to hundreds of questions that would need to be answered affirmatively along the path to product introduction. And when an answer was negative, then management needed to make the decision as to whether to agree to an "exception" and proceed into the next phase anyway, or to delay the project until the question was answered affirmatively.

Most people on our team reviewing HP's processes, and I think most engineers and middle managers involved in these processes, tended to look at these questions themselves as reasonable tests of readiness, but they missed a critical factor, which I insisted on bringing out explicitly.

I look at the product development process as a series of business risk reductions, ending when the product enters production with a minimum of problems. (The risks and consequences of problems will never be zero, so it's important to know what levels are acceptable.) You start at the beginning, with an idea for a new product. What do you know about it? Only your previous experience with similar products and technologies and some information about the market. Relative to the ultimate goal of introducing a successful, profitable product, what is the risk at this point? Everything. The entire future profit stream from that potential product is at risk. It may not materialize or may be compromised. The potential satisfied customers may not ever step forward. The potential new platform that the product represents may remain a fantasy. A whole new market may be missed.

So you take what you know, and you define some first steps in R&D that will increase your knowledge about the technology and the product, and maybe about the market. If you carry out these steps successfully, you will reduce the business risk by an increment. That sets you up to repeat the process, defining additional steps that will reduce the risk some more. From management's point of view, for each increment of program investment, the program activities are expected to achieve a specified reduction in business risk. And you do this repeatedly until you arrive at the product release to production.

As our updated process definition emerged at HP, we had identified nine phases of our Product Life Cycle Process:

- Concept – which begins with a Release to Concept meeting to establish a small team to conceptualize a new product, perhaps involving a bit of laboratory experimentation, and ends with the Release to Investigation
- Investigation – which involves initial technical and market analysis to quantify potential sales and technical risks, and ends with the Release to Definition
- Definition – which utilizes the results of the Investigation to establish preliminary product specifications, pricing, cost analysis, reliability, marketing and sales requirements, and so on, and ends with the release to Development
- Development – which involves the actual development of the product in accordance with the Definition, and ends with the

Release to Qualification

- Qualification – which utilizes technical data from product prototypes to ensure that the product would likely meet the requirements specified in the Definition, with particular emphasis on reliability and regulatory compliance, and ends with the Release to First Production
- First Production – which provides for the operation of the production line to produce the first shippable units, including standard and extra testing, and ends with the Release to Shipment
- Shipment – when products are first shipped to customers, so beginning the production phase of the product's life cycle
- Discontinuance – which involves the myriad decisions and actions to be taken when a product is no longer going to be produced for sale, and ends with the Release to Support Life
- Support Life – which is the final phase of the product's life cycle, in which units in the field are supported with repair, calibration and other services for a number of years following Discontinuance, and ends with a Product Obsolescence meeting, involving a full retrospective review of the entire program

The details of these phase definitions don't matter as much as the concepts, and the systems available today can be used to good effect. What I particularly liked conceptually about the HP system in its time was that it provided a structure for the entire life cycle and included the retrospective at the end, so that even years after the Release to Concept, lessons could be learned from the program. The other thing I liked was that the release criteria and meetings were clearly focused on prospective analysis of the remaining risks in the program, with full awareness that the choice to make the necessary incremental investment in each phase was a business decision deserving the most sober analysis. In that process, although the meetings would be heavy in technical content, they were never to be just technical meetings, but unmistakably business meetings.

As Mr. Reinertsen's text points out, these phases generally do not proceed completely independently in the real world. Activities from one phase often proceed in parallel with activities from a different phase, whether top management wants them to or not. This happens as a natural consequence of intelligent decision-making about acceptance of minor, constrained risk in favor of reducing overall development cycle time and program risk. The result, especially in the context of multiple ongoing product development projects, can be an overall improvement in the expected value of that investment portfolio. It is also a recognition that, in a creative process like product development, variability cannot and should not be limited in the same way that is appropriate in the repetitive processes of manufacturing, for example.

It is worth reviewing, in this context, how the practice of engineering has evolved. Over the four decades since I became an engineer, the breadth of the typical engineering job has shrunken. There is less focus on hardware and more on software, not just in the products themselves but also in the tools available for applied research and product development. Prototyping and manufacturing increasingly use additive manufacturing, such as 3D printing, which involves a heavy component of software and digital models. Aerodynamics R&D used to rely far more heavily on wind-tunnel testing than in today's world, where computational capabilities have lent high accuracy and flexibility to computational fluid dynamic simulations. What once took me days with pencil and paper, slide rule, strip-chart recorders and bulky test equipment can be done in minutes or hours with a computer and advanced, miniaturized instrumentation. In the waning days of my career with HP, I was astounded and excited by the emerging capability of software to emulate the behavior of measurement instruments. It seemed that an entire communications product development effort could be driven primarily by software. And this engineering world continues to evolve at an increasing pace.

Thus, even more than in the past, one of the most important factors to consider in planning a product development is the concept of disruption. Disruption fundamentally means the rapid obsolescence of the status quo in technology or business models by means of qualitatively different technology or business models. Examples are beyond number. Decades ago, steam-driven earth-moving equipment was rather suddenly rendered obsolete by hydraulic machinery. More recently, video disk technology quickly supplanted VHS magnetic tape technology. Music on CDs is giving way to files stored on phones and other devices. Television is giving way to streaming media. C8 MediSensors intended to disrupt the diabetes treatment industry with a completely new technology that promised to be better in many ways and less expensive than existing technologies. An excellent, although somewhat dated, discussion of how disruption usually happens, and why it has been difficult traditionally for an organization to disrupt its own products or business models, is provided in *The Innovator's Dilemma*, by Clayton M. Christensen.[18]

Especially in today's world, where technology changes at lightning speed even as compared with the pace of ten or fifteen years ago, it is highly likely that a disruptive technology or business model will emerge during the anticipated lifetime of the product being planned. If the disruption happens soon enough, it can destroy the anticipated return on investment in the planned product.

In the context of planning a product's life cycle, this factor drives all milestones and phases to occur more swiftly than in the past. Consequently, the life cycle management processes described above are gradually giving way to much more streamlined methods. In particular, phase reviews and releases may be collapsed into fewer events and may take different forms than the traditional meetings. Software developments involve substantially different phase definitions. Nevertheless, all phases, including the entire production phase, are shorter and shorter. Even in the 1990s, I recall attending meetings at Compaq Computer for a potential consultancy, and gaining an understanding that their laptop computer products, at the time, had a manufacturing life of just three months before the next model filled the factory.

Today's even faster pace of change also prompts much more emphasis on competitive scanning and anticipation of technological change. And it puts even stronger emphasis on an organization's ability to disrupt its own products, technologies and business models. This pace still varies among industries and technologies, as it did in the past, but none is immune to outside disruption, and all ought to be planning for self-disruption.

In the slower times when we developed the new Product Life Cycle Process for HP's Test and Measurement business, one of the business concepts that came to the fore was the "minimum viable product," or MVP. The idea was to identify exactly what the market needed technically in the near future, and what technical features would meet those needs without excess. Aiming at such a result would tend to minimize technical risk and time in the development effort, while offering just the value that the market would be seeking at the point of product introduction. This approach moved the organization toward a business model in which the company would produce a continual stream of incrementally better products.

This MVP idea helped to focus the discussions, especially in the early phases of development, on business considerations. It was not lost on me that this idea was very similar to a position I had taken on the advanced development of magnetohydrodynamic (MHD) electric power generation technology in my earlier position in the utility industry, and so I can say that this principle applies to both incremental and advanced technology development.

Despite today's fast pace, it is comforting to know that the same principles embodied in HP's Product Life Cycle Process back then are still valid today. It's just that the planning and execution must happen faster.

And speaking of disruption, it is worth mentioning that the business model of US defense contracting has evolved substantially in the years following my 2005 work at Raytheon Missile Systems. For several years, ending in 2009, there was an increasing trend to "combination" contracts, in which there was an untracked mix of fixed-price and cost-plus components. This was found to be at odds with the desire to achieve increasing cost-efficiency in government contracting,[19] as articulated in a 2009 Presidential order.[20] By 2013, due to a directed effort toward more competitive and fixed-price contracting, that trend had reversed, and about two-thirds of defense contracts were fixed-price.[21] Some of this trend has affected research, development, test and evaluation (RDT&E) contracting, but the generally available literature has not yet made clear whether or how the shift has broadly affected the management of risk during system development. One would hope for a stronger focus on risk reduction throughout R&D, with an eye toward production. However, anecdotally, the reality in defense contracting has been that the armed services are tending to contract for non-developmental, capability-based contracts, rather than requirements-driven contracts, thereby shifting risk from the government to the contractors.[22]

Now, with that background, let's look in more detail at product development as an exercise in risk reduction. Let's suppose you've followed an effective process to develop the product. At the point of production release, what residual business risk remains? If everything has gone well, the critical uncertainties that existed at the beginning of the program have been resolved, and the only risks that remain are the normal production risks, consisting of everyday process upsets like temporary shortages of parts, discovery of defective components on the production line, process equipment outages, and so on. One can rather easily characterize, measure and even predict those risks.

These business risks, whether the programmatic risks that exist at the beginning of the development program, or the production risks remaining at the end of the program, might be expressed as dollars (or another currency, of course). At the beginning of the program, it may not be easy to be precise in such an estimate, but it is valuable to make the effort, and even more so, to refresh the estimate of remaining risks as the program proceeds.

Imagine that the development team has reached the ostensible end of a particular phase of the development program. The team is looking for an executive decision to release the program to proceed into the next phase, that is, to pass through a release gate. As suggested above, the team is asking for a decision to invest another increment of money (increments that grow substantially with each phase until product release) in the hope of further reducing total business risk by a pre-determined amount. The decision-makers will consider how much the original risks have been reduced up to the current point (i.e., the track record of the team), what risks are to be eliminated in the next phase, and how much money will be required to accomplish that. This was the critical perception that had been largely missing in the way HP teams prepared for phase release meetings prior to our team's redefinition of the process. In the new process, the meetings were to be structured to answer those business questions.

So we can imagine a quantity that we call "business risk," the sum of all the various kinds of risk, that begins with a relatively high value at the beginning of a development program and ends with the relatively low residual risk that is acceptable for the production operation to assume and manage.

Note that as we proceed through the development program by means of staged investments, the risk generally is reduced in a non-linear fashion. The early investigations will generally reduce risk by only small amounts, as preliminary market investigations are performed, laboratory tests are undertaken and conceptual designs are produced. And in the late stages of development, when readiness for production is being established, the business risk again is reduced by a small amount for a given investment, since most of the risk has already been eliminated in the intervening phases. This means that the intervening phases generally are characterized by rather steep risk reduction, at least in principle. So if we were to plot the business risk profile over the course of the development program, it could be expected to follow an "S" shape, as illustrated in Figure A-1.

Let's come back for a moment to the definition of business risk. We could have called it "technical risk," which is the term that many R&D teams are used to using. But my contention is that any risk is ultimately a business risk. If a company is about to commit some millions of dollars to a development that may fail, then that money is at risk. If a company foresees a new market worth billions of dollars in potential future profits, all hinging on a successful development, then those billions are at risk. These are two ends of the spectrum of potential monetary definitions of business risk, and what's appropriate to use in a particular situation depends on the nature of the development and the objectives of the organization. For our purposes here, the conceptual idea is sufficient.

Implied in this discussion is the fact that the business risks can be classified as either "market" risks, in the sense that the product may not sell as well as expected or may otherwise fall short of expectations in the marketplace, and "implementation" risks,

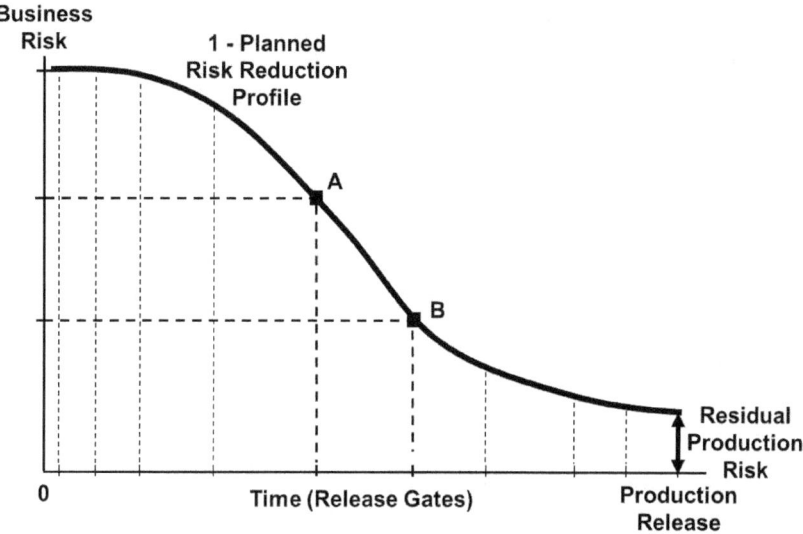

Figure A-1

Product development as a business risk reduction process.
The intention of a product development program is to reduce business risk incrementally, by means of incremental investments in development. Each increment of investment is committed at the time of a program phase release or "gate." Having achieved point A, management is faced with an investment decision to attempt to reach point B. The objective is that, at the time of production release, only residual production risk remains.

having to do with the product technology, design, manufacturing processes, component quality, logistics, and so on. The discussion that follows is focused on implementation risks, because that is where my work with Raytheon Missile Systems was focused. Nevertheless, analogous discussion is certainly possible for the planning of market risk reduction.[23]

At the missile factory, I illustrated the problem to the executives by showing them something like Figure A-2, which portrays what I call "letting the risk roll downhill into production." At each gate, management implicitly judged remaining business risk to be on line 1, when in fact, it was following something like line 2. Risks were remaining higher than planned throughout the development program, resulting in an excess of risk at the time of production release. The excess risk inevitably showed up as excess production cost, since risks inexorably materialize into real problems in production.

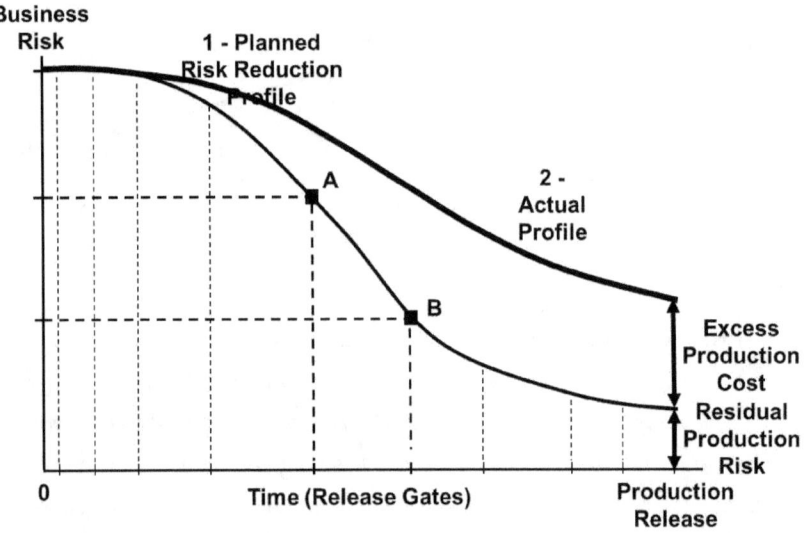

Figure A-2
Letting the risk roll downhill into production.
In many development programs, business risk reduction does not follow the intended profile. Risks are not fully resolved as planned at each release gate. The result is that, at production release, the business risk exceeds the normal residual production risk, leading inexorably to greater-than-expected production costs.

In this particular organization, the fact that risk was running higher than expected throughout development was remaining unrecognized by the management team during each program, thereby constituting a systemic measurement error that increased over time in the program. This concept is illustrated in Figure A-3.

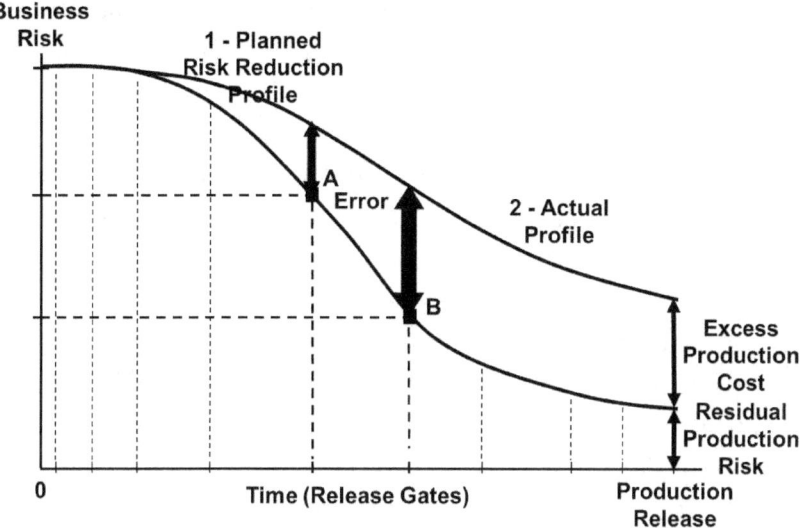

Figure A-3
Systemic error in risk measurement.
The culture and processes of a development organization may incorporate systemic error in the measurement of remaining business risk over the course of a development program.

The reasons for this systemic measurement error were rooted in the organization's culture and processes. This is understandable in the following way. Release gates generally take the form of review meetings, in which managers representing general management, R&D, manufacturing, marketing, quality and other functions view presentations by members of the development team. These presentations usually are structured around the phase release criteria, so the audience will be exposed to a stream of technical information.

In the end, such meetings are primarily visual inspections of meta-data and are unavoidably subjective to some extent. They may be suffused with aspirations of the technical team, management pressures to move the program along its path, interpersonal strife that affects the presentation and interpretation of the data, and perhaps other factors detrimental to objective analysis. These factors can easily lead to a lack of disclosure or understatement of problems. Thus, such factors can be sources of systemic error in risk measurement over the course of a development program. One important part of the solution lies in identifying and employing more objective measurement methods to displace subjective ones, and that is generally a substantial challenge.

Even more important, I think, is to create a culture that *encourages* participants to speak even the harshest truth about the risks at hand. The history of business and technology is rife with examples of organizations that effectively silenced truthful disclosure and open consideration of risks that later proved to be unacceptable. It ought not to take an act of exceptional courage for an employee or a manager to expose an unresolved risk, and one of the most important functions of leadership is to create an environment of low barriers to that kind of disclosure. *The courage ought to show in the leadership's intention, commitment and action to create such a culture. This is what we ought to expect of organizational leaders.*

Now, the foregoing discussion is not to say that every "exception" to expected risk reduction, or every deviation from the planned risk reduction profile, is symptomatic of a systemic measurement error. Managers commonly recognize that certain release criteria have not been met (an exception) and make the decision to proceed into the next phase anyway, with the understanding that the exception will be resolved at a later time. The occasional prudent decision to accept a continued risk doesn't necessarily represent a process problem. It's a pattern of unrecognized risk that is symptomatic.

It's often said that it's important to make mistakes early in the development, rather than later, and this can be a valid approach to eliminating or mitigating risks at low cost, as compared with postponing such efforts until later in the program, or with discovering an insurmountable development barrier later than it might have been found. In our conceptual model, this approach would result in a steeper slope of the risk reduction profile in the early phases. Such investment decisions are not always simple, however, as they often involve difficult trade-offs of how best to invest scarce capital in the early phases.

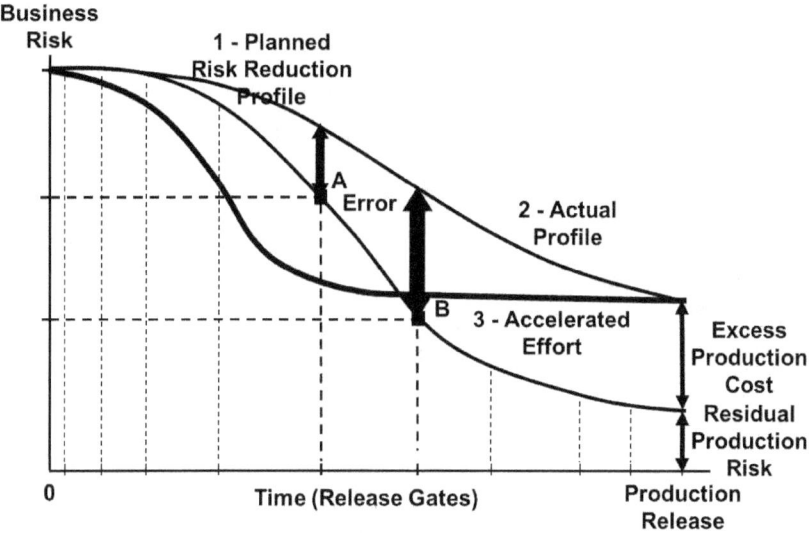

Figure A-4

Attempted faster development doesn't necessarily solve the problem. *On its own, investing in doing the same steps more efficiently doesn't necessarily lead to decreased risk later in the program.*

Meanwhile, it's worth cautioning that, in the effort to get things done faster in development, it is not always helpful to accelerate gating processes themselves. Just trying to do the same gating process steps more quickly may not result in lower risk. Instead, the result may be a faster arrival at a similarly unsatisfactory production risk level, as illustrated in Figure A-4. Lower risk at production release must come from doing different things, such as more

192

effective investment in risk reduction and more effective gating reviews.

So, whatever the shape of line 1, representing the planned risk-reduction profile, the challenge is to hold to that curve and avoid stumbling onto line 2. A focus on accurate risk measurement becomes critical to improvement.

It is also important to recognize that even more benefit can come from reducing the level of risk at the beginning of the program. A reduction in initial risk implies an increase in the relevant knowledge available before the program starts. This is illustrated by the more ideal line 4 in Figure A-5.

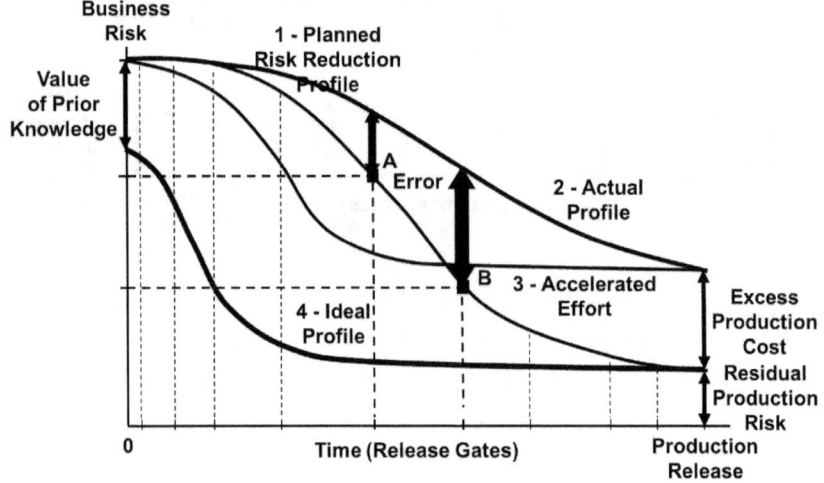

Figure A-5
The value of prior knowledge.
An increase in prior knowledge decreases the remaining risk to be resolved during the program and represents a valuable investment.

Note that the reduction in initial risk represents the value of prior knowledge, which can be an excellent investment for the organization. This is the foundation for applied R&D, for example.

Naturally, achieving a development result something like the ideal line 4 in Figure A-5 implies that the project could reach production release much sooner, or contrarily, the project could be started later and still achieve the same release date. In either case, overall business risk has been reduced.

Both initial market risk and initial product implementation risk can be reduced through prior knowledge. Such market risk reduction is the underlying subject of any number of texts and courses within the marketing discipline. For the purpose of the current discussion, we will maintain our focus on implementation risk.

There are generally three sources of relevant prior knowledge that can reduce initial implementation risk: statistical characterization of production processes and product design margins; continuous anticipation of production process capability requirements to accommodate evolving customer needs and product technologies; and optimization of the role and strategy of test as an information source for measuring risk.

Statistical characterization and process control are well-established methodologies in modern manufacturing. They can be a tremendous challenge in an environment of high-mix, low-volume products, such as communications satellites or military missiles. Creativity is needed in such environments to be able to apply the lessons from volume manufacturing.

Process capability represents, in statistical terms, the process's ability to produce products that are nearly all within the range of the performance specifications for the product. If process variability is too high, the process will produce an unacceptable number of products falling outside the specifications. It is important for the organization to be looking ahead at what process capability improvements will be needed in order to produce future products meeting evolving customer needs and incorporating new technologies.

Regarding the role and strategy of testing, it is critical to recognize that risk measurement via subjective reviews has proven to be an unreliable process, and that testing may increase the objectivity of risk measurement in this context. Hence, the importance of effective, reliable test processes and equipment, and effective use of the information produced by testing. The test methodology and use of test information should be determined before the relevant program phase begins, so that the methodology will not be corrupted by external pressures.

So far we have discussed the product development life cycle in the sense that it might apply to a brand new product. But what about incremental design changes to an existing product, or other projects of conceptually smaller scope? It should come as no surprise that the same principles apply, and it is up to the project team and the organization leaders to determine whether any phases or release criteria of the life cycle plan ought to be skipped. It's been my observation that there is great benefit in maintaining the defined product life cycle process even in such cases. Doing so maintains process discipline and ensures that no potentially important criteria are overlooked, and it can bring out risks that affect not only the current project but also existing related products. In the worst case, some time is spent deciding that particular criteria don't apply, or that a particular phase (say, Concept) has been obviated.

An underlying theme of the foregoing discussion on product development and risk is that every meeting that occurs during the development cycle, whether the presenting topic is technology, budget, or anything else, is a business meeting. The decisions that are made in each meeting will affect either the definition of the development risk profile or the progress of the program along its planned profile. Keeping this fact in mind ought to encourage healthier decision-making and more open communication among program participants and management.

APPENDIX B:
DOROTHY'S TRAVEL GUIDE
TO THE YELLOW BRICK ROAD

No one can predict what steep hills, blind turns, friends, adversaries and challenging adventures you will encounter along your own Yellow Brick Road. The ideas that follow are offered as general guideposts along the way. You may find that these do not differ so greatly among the various roles that you may fill during your journey.

The First-Level Supervisor

Day by day, you must focus on the needs of the business and the objectives for which you are responsible. Be aware that you will not succeed in the long run by coming up with all the answers yourself. Find ways to engage the knowledge and wisdom of your team members. As you do so, you will make your job easier.

You may feel like a babysitter sometimes. Remember that if you act that way, then that is exactly what you are. Do not tolerate childishness among your team members. But just as with disciplining children, do not rebuke them in public. I have noticed that when supervisors do such a thing, they only diminish themselves as leaders and lose the confidence of their subordinates. You will succeed by treating your people with respect, and that includes not settling for less than respectable behavior from them. In doing so, you will unavoidably demonstrate human love and compassion, although that fact will, appropriately, remain unspoken.

When interpersonal conflict arises, act to focus on the process involved, not the people. When the process becomes the issue, rather than interpersonal relationships, then you can usually diffuse the situation and put it on a productive track. I have found it effective sometimes, when tempers are running high, to simply take the blame for the problem upon myself. The processes are ultimately the leader's responsibility, after all. I recall once stopping an escalating argument between an engineer and a materials inspector in my department over some minor matter by simply saying, "You know, guys, this problem is my fault. I set up the situation inadvertently. There's no reason for you two to be angry with each other. If anything, you ought to be angry with me. Let's sit down and figure out what the process ought to be." They both looked at me in stunned silence, and then we sat down and had a reasonable discussion. I was pleased with how quickly they had calmed down, and I remembered that tactic.

People take all kinds of risks, whether asked or not. If the people are unmotivated or demoralized, those risks will often be immature, selfish or destructive to others. But when the people are focused on constructive business objectives, then they will be more likely to take risks that are well-considered and generous to the team. Their sensible risk-taking in support of business objectives is to be celebrated. You can help them reach this point by honestly recognizing their concerns, helping them to solve those, and inviting them on to the next level. As you do so, they will begin to draw on their individual reserves of courage. In the process, you will learn the nature and limits of each person's courage.

A little bit of chaos will always creep into any organization. You won't quite control everything, and that's not a bad thing, because those patches of chaos can serve as centers of creativity and innovation. But while a bit of chaos is acceptable, surprises are not. A key to success in tolerating that chaos is to be sure that the team is fully educated on the technical and business implications of their work. The more they understand, the better their decisions will be about how to communicate about their efforts.

Likewise, seek to understand as much as you can about the business. Be certain that you understand what your manager expects of you, and understand his or her business objectives, as well as those of at least the next level of management. Always be prepared to show how your decisions and actions support those objectives, especially when it might not be readily apparent. Create and present metrics that are as simple as possible, fully support the mission, and drive the appropriate improvement. Where there is ambiguity, and there always will be some, remain calm and flexible. Be ready to shift when the unexpected happens, for you can be sure that it will happen.

Paying attention to others' communication styles is important to your success. Present your information as concisely as possible, especially to your manager, but understand that people naturally communicate in different ways. You are wise to adjust your communication style to match, as best you can. Your manager may want conclusions first and supporting data after or, instead, may want you to start relating the necessary information from the beginning and finish with the conclusion, like a story unfolding. If your manager tends to show a lot of emotion or very little, it is usually best to adjust your own communication likewise, in some measure, without sacrificing your authenticity.

Remember that your manager is looking openly for your knowledge, wisdom and courage and, at least implicitly, the qualities of love and compassion that you bring to your job. In every interaction with management, you are selling them on you. Be yourself, and remember that there are only rare exceptions to the rule that your manager wants you to succeed.

The Middle Manager

Your first duty is to focus on the business objectives, as it is for the supervisors who report to you. In doing so, you take the role of a knowledgeable, compassionate and courageous coach for them. You must provide challenging goals aimed at improving the ways in which your department works. Are the processes well-defined and well-controlled? Are they producing the quality of results that's desired? Are they designed for cycle time? Begin with the fundamentals, such as how jobs are defined, how people are hired, how the team is organized, and how objectives are set. Engage your own knowledge and wisdom, but seek and nurture that of your team members.

Observe how the supervisors lead their teams, and provide coaching in a firm but respectful way. Expect that they will resolve employee performance issues in a thoughtful and expeditious manner, keeping the performance and well-being of the team foremost in importance.

Maintain open lines of communication within the department. Practice the art of Management by Walking Around. Beyond the day-to-day objectives, these are ways of showing that you care about the people and their struggles. And you must care sincerely.

Seek to understand as much as you can about the business, and demonstrate that knowledge in your leadership of your department.

Have the courage to fully understand your manager's objectives by questioning them carefully and, if you have concerns, by going higher up in the organization for clarification. Contribute to that discussion from your knowledge and wisdom and your commitment to your team's success.

Meanwhile, support your peers in the achievement of their objectives. Demonstrate to your management, through your focus and communication, your commitment to the organization's success and your contribution to it.

Remember to communicate upward in terminology that the upper management uses to assess the business. This means less technical detail and more focus on operational and financial metrics.

The Senior Manager or Executive

You bear significant or primary responsibility for your business's success. A mistake on your part can have significant business impact on the company and its value net – customers, suppliers, competitors, and complementers.[24] A mistake can demoralize members of your organization and cause them to lose confidence in you. Your knowledge and wisdom are tested every moment, and the decisions you make are dependent on the information you gain from your team, and their own knowledge and wisdom. Test your knowledge and theirs relentlessly.

Show the same care for each team member that you did as a first-line supervisor and as a middle manager. Set the example of how to incorporate the fundamental values of human love and compassion into the business in ways that make it more successful.

Day-by-day, demonstrate a firm grasp of the direction of the organization. What is true north? Drive organizational alignment through clear communication, including Management by Walking Around. Have the courage to invite discussion and accept respectful dissent, for those are opportunities to leverage the knowledge and wisdom of your team, to make sensible adjustments to objectives and plans, and to reinforce organizational alignment.

Lead with integrity of intent, commitment, thought and action. Especially demonstrate those qualities in communicating to executives and your board of directors, because flaws in these qualities among senior or executive management can be fatal to an organization. If you are the CEO or another executive who interacts with the board, seek to develop a deep understanding of the board's intentions and concerns, and help its members to appreciate management's leadership and control of the organization through effective communication of plans and results.

Show the same care in interacting with customers, suppliers, and other business partners, as well as competitors. Your company's reputation and future are at stake.

The Small Business Owner

You may fill the roles of first-line supervisor, middle manager, senior manager and executive. Your commitment to your business is complete. You risk everything, every day. Your Yellow Brick Road is an exhilarating one.

You have an advantage over leaders in larger organizations, in that you can generally see the results of your efforts more readily and more quickly. You can be nimble with relative ease. That is something that leaders in large organizations must strive mightily to achieve.

But you have the disadvantage of not having other managers at hand to serve as sounding boards for your ideas. You may seek such a resource through local organizations of business owners, through consultants, or through mentors that you have come to trust. Self-reliance is a part of the nature of your work, but you must not let it become a trap.

Every landmark cited above for other kinds of managers is one that you must note. Most importantly, you must rely on your knowledge and wisdom, but you must test them relentlessly. Engage your employees in that process. This demands intellectual, social and emotional courage, and perhaps even moral courage occasionally.

Every customer is your boss. The best way to sell something to that customer is to show how your product or service meets their need better than any other, whether that need is functional or emotional. You cannot do so effectively without making the effort to understand those needs. Making that effort, over and over, will be burdensome unless you choose to regard it as fun. The best salespeople demonstrate a sincere interest in each customer as a person, and the sale becomes an outgrowth of that relationship. This is true in principle whether you're running a neighborhood grocery store or an online shopping service. It is not an overstatement to say that doing this with sincerity demands your love, compassion and courage, along with your knowledge and wisdom.

The Freelancer

You are part of that burgeoning segment of the workforce that does not associate exclusively with one organization. In the case of each client, your view of the leadership team will depend on the organizational level and element with which you contract and work. In some sense, you are the ultimate small business owner: You are your own business. Consequently, this section will sound a lot like that one.

You may not officially supervise any employee at all, or you may find yourself in the temporary role of a consulting manager or executive, with considerable responsibility. Given that breadth of possibilities, it is valuable to try to understand the landscape that we've explored above for each of the management roles. Even if you do not supervise others, it will benefit you to understand how those who supervise you view their own landscapes.

You may not enjoy the nimble environment that the small business owner has. But you will have the ability to seek others within the organization as sounding boards for your ideas, and that is an advantage.

As with the small business owner, you must rely on your knowledge and wisdom, but you must test them relentlessly. Engage your client and coworkers in that process. This demands intellectual, social and emotional courage, and perhaps even moral courage occasionally.

Every client is your boss. The best way to sell your services to that client is to show how your service meets their need better than any other. You cannot do so effectively without making the effort to understand those needs. Making that effort, over and over, will be burdensome unless you choose to regard it as fun. Adopt and demonstrate a sincere interest in each client as a person and in their organization as if it were your own. This is best done by engaging your love, compassion and courage, along with your knowledge and wisdom.

***

Now that we have explored how the attributes of leadership are best manifested in various management roles, you have the tools to extend this thinking to other leadership environments or non-leadership roles of interest to you.

APPENDIX C:
A SYNOPSIS OF "THE WIZARD OF OZ"

It's probably worth noting that the movie's story is not exactly the same as in L. Frank Baum's book, originally published in 1900, *The Wonderful Wizard of Oz*.[25] The book is widely regarded as a populist political allegory of the time. Despite plot differences from the book, the movie shares that interpretation and has also been described as psychological or religious allegory. However, for our purposes, we employ a direct interpretation of the characters as they present themselves in the movie, but we draw out their underlying lessons relating to leadership.

The story begins on a family farm in the vast plains of the state of Kansas, in America, in the early 1900s. The film images are presented in sepia tones, to impart the drabness of existence in that time and place. Young Dorothy Gale lives there with her Uncle Henry and Aunt Em, as well as her dog Toto and several farm hands. The drama begins when Toto bites a mean neighbor, is taken away to be euthanized, escapes and returns to Dorothy. Already feeling that her family and friends are neglecting her and that her life lacks adventure, Dorothy decides to run away from home with Toto, in order to protect him.

On the road, Dorothy and Toto encounter an itinerant fortune teller, who is a middle-aged phony but a fundamentally compassionate man. He surmises that she has run away from home, tricks her into believing that her aunt is terribly ill from grief at Dorothy's departure, and so convinces Dorothy to return home. But before she can get there, a powerful cyclone strikes the area. Unable to find Dorothy, her family and friends lock themselves in the storm cellar. Dorothy is forced to take shelter in the house. When the cyclone engulfs the house, Dorothy is struck on the head by flying debris and is knocked unconscious. Apparently delirious, she experiences the entire house being lifted by the cyclone.

When Dorothy believes that she has awakened, she finds that the house has arrived in the Land of Oz, a place full of strange and wonderful people and beings, where everything appears in vivid color. Specifically, she is in Munchkinland, where the little Munchkin people live. It so happens that her house has landed upon and killed the Wicked Witch of the East, who had terrorized the Munchkins. Dorothy is hailed as a heroine.

The Good Witch of the North, Glinda, arrives and inquires whether Dorothy is a good witch or a bad witch, and how she came to be in Oz. Dorothy claims not to be a witch and describes the cyclone.

Just then, the late witch's sister, the Wicked Witch of the West, arrives to claim the Ruby Slippers from her dead sister's feet. The slippers hold magical powers and cannot be removed while the wearer lives. In the nick of time, Glinda transfers the slippers to Dorothy's feet. The Wicked Witch of the West, who resembles Dorothy's mean neighbor in Kansas, departs after vowing to kill Dorothy and Toto and claim the slippers.

Dorothy tells Glinda of her one desire, to return home. Glinda tells her that she may find help from the great Wizard of Oz, who lives in the Emerald City. She instructs Dorothy to follow the Yellow Brick Road, which begins nearby, to reach the city.

Along the way, Dorothy encounters a Scarecrow made of straw stuffed into clothing, who is alive and feels that he is ignorant and incapable because he lacks a brain. Dorothy encourages him to accompany her to see the Wizard in hopes of obtaining a brain. Later, they encounter a Tin Man, who desires a heart, and a Cowardly Lion, who desires courage. These three characters bear resemblance to the farm hands at Dorothy's home. All of them proceed down the road in the hope that the Wizard will fulfill their desires.

The Wicked Witch of the West tries to stop the group in various ways but fails. In these encounters and later ones, the Scarecrow demonstrates wise insight and knowledge, the Tin Man demonstrates his compassion, and the Cowardly Lion shows great courage, all despite their perceived lack of these qualities.

Reaching the Emerald City, they are granted an audience with the Wizard, who appears as a frightful, ghostly head surrounded by flames. Before granting their wishes, the Wizard requires the travelers to prove their worth by bringing him the broomstick of the Wicked Witch of the West, with which she would not part while alive.

Heading to the witch's castle, the group is waylaid by the witch's servants, who are winged monkeys. Dorothy and Toto are carried off to the castle. While the witch prepares to kill Dorothy via a magic spell, Toto escapes, finds the Scarecrow, Tin Man and Cowardly Lion, and leads them back to the castle. They eventually free Dorothy, but the castle guards trap the group on the castle battlements. The witch arrives and sets fire to the Scarecrow, but Dorothy douses the flames with a bucket of water. The witch is also splashed with water and, as a result, dissolves in a puddle. The guards, relieved of the witch's tyranny, celebrate and award Dorothy the broomstick.

Having returned to the Emerald City, the group presents the broomstick to the Wizard, but he balks at granting their wishes. While the group protests to no avail, Toto pulls back a nearby curtain, revealing the Wizard to be simply a man who bears a close resemblance to the fortune teller that Dorothy had encountered before the cyclone hit. He has been using a machine to generate the frightful Wizard image.

Contrite, he admits to his deceit. But he demonstrates his own compassion and wisdom by showing the Scarecrow that he lacks only a symbol of knowledge, in the form of a diploma, which the Wizard then gives to the Scarecrow, thereby unleashing his knowledge and wisdom. Similarly, he provides the Tin Man with a heart-shaped clock that ticks out a beat, and he provides the Cowardly Lion with a medal for courage.

For Dorothy, the Wizard offers to take her back to Kansas aboard the same hot-air balloon that had deposited him in Oz many years before. Unfortunately, at the last moment, Dorothy and Toto are left behind as the balloon ascends with the Wizard aboard. Dorothy pleads with him to come back, but he responds, "I can't come back! I don't know how it works!"

Dorothy is desolate, until Glinda arrives and explains that all she needs to do is to tap the heels of the Ruby Slippers together three times, while repeating, "There's no place like home." After bidding farewell to her friends, Dorothy does so and wakes up in her own bed, surrounded by her family and friends, as well as Toto and the fortune teller. She realizes that this is where she belongs, after all, and says again, "There's no place like home."

REFERENCES

[1] Correspondence with Sonya Sepahban, Senior Vice President, General Dynamics (Retired), 2015

[2] Salovey, Peter, and Mayer, John, "Emotional Intelligence," Imagination, Cognition, and Personality, vol. 9, pp 185-121, 1990

[3] Goleman, Daniel, *Emotional Intelligence*, 10th Anniversary Edition, Bantam Books, New York, 2006

[4] Zygielbaum, P.S., and Dolbec, A. C., "Magnetohydrodynamics: An Engineering Perspective," IEEE Transactions on Power Apparatus and Systems, Vol. PAS-100, No. 5, May 1981, pp. 2529-2538

[5] Borror, Connie M., Editor, *The Certified Quality Engineer Handbook*, Third Edition, ASQ Quality Press, 2009, pp. 321–332

[6] Correspondence with Dr. Scott S. Elliott, R&D and manufacturing executive and consultant, 2015

[7] Goldratt, Eliyahu M., *The Goal*, Second Revised Edition, North River Press, Great Barrington, MA, 1992

[8] Schonberger, Richard J., *World Class Manufacturing*, The Free Press, New York, 1986

[9] Reinertsen, Donald G., *The Principles of Product Development Flow: Second Generation Lean Product Development*, Celeritas Publishing, Redondo Beach, CA, 2009

[10] www.ctesonomacounty.org

[11] Packard, David, *The HP Way*, HarperCollins Publishers, New York, 1995

[12] Teal, Thomas, *First Person: Tales of Management Courage and Tenacity*, Harvard Business School Publishing, Boston, 1996

[13] Drucker, Peter F., "What Executives Should Remember," Harvard Business Review, Vol. 84, No. 2, February 2006

[14] Isaacson, Walter, *Steve Jobs*, Simon & Schuster Paperbacks, New York, 2013

[15] Welch, Jack, with Byrne, John A., *Jack: Straight from the Gut*, Warner Business Books, New York, 2001

[16] Kennedy, John F., *Profiles in Courage*, Harper Perennial, New York, 2006

[17] www.lionswhiskers.com

[18] Christensen, Clayton M., *The Innovator's Dilemma*, Reprint Edition, HarperBusiness, New York, 2011

[19] Ellman, Jesse, et al., "Defense Contract Trends: U.S. Department of Defense Contract Spending and the Supporting Industrial Base," Center for Strategic and International Studies Defense-Industrial Initiatives Group, Rowman & Littlefield, May 2011

[20] Obama, Barack, "Memorandum for the Heads of Executive Departments and Agencies. Subject: Government Contracting," White House, Washington DC, 2009

[21] Ellman, Jesse, et al., "U.S. Department of Defense Contract Spending and the Industrial Base, 2000-2013," Center for Strategic and International Studies Defense-Industrial Initiatives Group, Rowman & Littlefield, October 2014

[22] Correspondence with Ms. Sonya Sepahban, Senior Vice President, General Dynamics (Retired), 2016

[23] Correspondence with Mr. Larry Pendergrass, R&D executive and consultant, 2016

[24] Brandenberger, Adam M., and Nalebuff, Barry J., *Co-opetition*, New York, Doubleday, 1997

[25] Baum, L. Frank, *The Wonderful Wizard of Oz*, 100th Anniversary Edition, HarperCollins, New York, 2000

ABOUT THE AUTHOR

Paul S. Zygielbaum has over 40 years' professional leadership experience in engineering, manufacturing, operations, sales, strategic business development, and executive consulting. His contributions span the aerospace, electric utility, electronic communications and biomedical device industries. He is known for turning around troubled businesses.

Most recently, Mr. Zygielbaum was a co-founder, member of the board, and CEO and president of C8 MediSensors, a medical device startup, from which position he retired in 2013.

Mr. Zygielbaum has served as a volunteer on technical committees and boards of various engineering societies and on boards and committees of various non-profit human service and educational organizations. As a long-term survivor of mesothelioma, he is also a noted advocate for the rights of asbestos-poisoning victims, for banning the commercial use of asbestos, and for improving medical treatments for patients.

Mr. Zygielbaum holds advanced degrees in engineering and business. He has published over 20 technical journal papers, reviews and articles in the fields of aerospace and energy technologies and public health.

Mr. Zygielbaum and his wife, Michelle, reside in California. They enjoy their family of three grown children and six grandchildren, travel extensively, and serve on the boards of local non-profit organizations.

www.leadingfromcourage.com